Acclaim for
33 Days to Merciful Love

Within the pages of *33 Days to Merciful Love* lies an earth-shattering insight, certifying its place among the most important books of our generation. It is this: As an age, with a river of heinous sin overflowing the banks of humanity, we have quite simply exhausted our reparative capacity to sate the demands of Divine Justice. Seeing this very moment from the Cross, Merciful Love willed a new age in Salvation History to coincide with the dawn of the third Christian millennium. An Age of Divine Mercy. An Age when all people can appeal to Perfect Mercy without fear of Perfect Justice. With exquisite timing in this Jubilee Year, Fr. Michael Gaitley shows us the power of just such an offering to Merciful Love in the lives of the greatest saints of our time, methodically prepares us to follow their lead, and reveals what it can mean to us and the men and women of our time if and when we do.

— **Brian J. Gail**
Catholic Speaker and Bestselling Author

33 Days to Merciful Love

A Do-It-Yourself Retreat in Preparation for Consecration to Divine Mercy

Fr. Michael E. Gaitley, MIC

2017

Available from:
Marian Helpers Center
Stockbridge, MA 01263

Prayerline: 1-800-804-3823
marian.org

Orderline: 1-800-462-7426
shopmercy.org

IMPRIMI POTEST:
Very Rev. Kazimierz Chwalek, MIC
Provincial Superior
The Blessed Virgin Mary, Mother of Mercy Province
January 1, 2016

Library of Congress Catalog Number: 2016930904
ISBN: 978-1-59614-345-6
First edition (5th printing): 2017

Layout and page design: Kathy Szpak

Printed in the United States of America

To the Marian Missionaries of Divine Mercy

May we trust in Jesus even more.

My power is made perfect
in weakness.

—*Jesus*

Contents

In Gratitude

First off, I'd like to thank Fr. Chris Alar, MIC, and Mark Moran for reasons that will become clear in the introduction. Second, I feel deep gratitude to Fr. Marc Foley, OCD, whose brilliant course on Thérèse of Lisieux opened my eyes to hidden treasures buried in the saint's writings. Third, I'm grateful to all those who read drafts of this book and offered comments and suggestions, especially Sarah Chichester, Ann Diaz, Jane Cavolina, Chris Sparks, Felix Carroll, and David Came. Fourth, my thanks go out to all those who prayed for this work, particularly Sr. Mary John Paul Asemota, O. Praem., Fr. Greg Staab, OMV, and the Marian Missionaries of Divine Mercy (especially those at the Merrell Inn in Lee, Massachusetts). Finally, I'll be forever grateful to St. Thérèse herself for sending me the yellow roses that changed my life and for teaching me the Little Way of mercy that saved it.

Fr. Michael E. Gaitley, MIC, STL
National Shrine of The Divine Mercy
Stockbridge, Massachusetts
December 8, 2015
Solemnity of the Immaculate Conception
Beginning of the Jubilee Year of Mercy

Acknowledgements

Permission to cite from the following is gratefully acknowledged:

From *Story of a Soul*, translated by John Clarke, O.C.D. Copyright © 1975, 1976, 1996 by Washington Province of Discalced Carmelites ICS Publications 2131 Lincoln Road, N.E. Washington, DC 20002 U.S.A. www.icspublications.org

From *General Correspondence* Volume One translated by John Clarke, O.C.D. Copyright © 1982 by Washington, Province of Discalced Carmelites ICS Publications 2131 Lincoln Road, N.E. Washington, DC 20002 U.S.A. www.icspublications.org

From *General Correspondence* Volume Two translated by John Clarke, O.C.D. Copyright © 1988 by Washington Province of Discalced Carmelites ICS Publications 2131 Lincoln Road, N.E. Washington, DC 20002 U.S.A. www.icspublications.org

From *With Empty Hands* by Conrad de Meester, O.C.D. Copyright © 2002 by Washington Province of Discalced Carmelites ICS Publications 2131 Lincoln Road N.E. Washington, DC 20002 U.S.A. www.icspublications.org

INTRODUCTION
Meet Three Friends

I'd like to begin by introducing three friends.

PRIEST FRIEND: A CONSECRATION TO DIVINE MERCY. The first friend is Fr. Chris Alar, MIC, a priest in my community, the Marian Fathers of the Immaculate Conception.

One day, Fr. Chris burst into my office after having just offered Mass. He looked like he'd just seen a ghost, so I stopped what I was doing and gave him my full attention.

"Father Mike, do we have a consecration to Divine Mercy?"

"No. At least I don't think so," I replied.

"Well, we need one. During Mass, it hit me like a ton of bricks that we need a consecration to Divine Mercy, and I think you should write it. But if you don't, I will. I think it's really important, Mike. Nothing has ever hit me so strongly. I feel that the Lord really wants it."

It was clear to me that the Lord had spoken to Fr. Chris' heart. But I didn't feel that he was also speaking to my heart, asking me to write such a book. So, I told Fr. Chris that he'd have to do it.

COLLEGE FRIEND: A SEQUEL TO MARIAN CONSECRATION. The second friend is Mark Moran, an old buddy from college.

In a sense, Mark is one of the most important people in my life because he introduced me to the book that completely changed it.

It happened during my freshman year. I was walking to class, minding my own business, when Mark came up to me, basically shoved a book in my face, and said, "Gaitley, you've gotta read this!" With my heavy class load, I didn't have time for any extra reading, and I told him as much. Well, that didn't faze him. He kept pestering me. And so, not wanting to be late for class, I took the book.

The book is called *True Devotion to Mary* by St. Louis de Montfort, and it describes a path to holiness called "Marian consecration" or "a total consecration to Jesus through Mary."

Most important for me, de Montfort basically claimed that such a consecration is the *quickest* and *easiest* way to become a saint. Well, when I saw that claim on the back of the book, I was sold. After all, I figured that only the "quickest and easiest" path could help someone like me to become a saint. So, I followed de Montfort's recommendation and consecrated myself totally to Jesus through Mary, and my life has never been the same. Of course, I'm still no saint, but at least I have hope that it's possible.

I hardly heard from Mark after college. But then, one day earlier this year, he called me out of the blue. While it was great to hear from him, I had to tell him I couldn't talk because I was rushing to meet a book deadline the next day. Mark said, "No problem. But that's why I called." I asked him what he meant. He continued, "Well, I was just praying, and I felt an inspiration to call you, because I know what your next book needs to be."

I thought to myself, "I already know what the next book will be. It's going to be on St. Thérèse of Lisieux and her Little Way." Still, to humor him, I replied, "Oh, yeah, what book is that?"

For the second time, Mark changed my life. He said, *"You need to do for the Offering to Merciful Love of St. Thérèse of Lisieux what you did for Marian consecration.* That's all I wanted to tell you. Talk to you later."

With those words, the dots immediately connected. I thanked Mark and hung up the phone. But before I connect those dots for you, let me introduce a third friend.

Saint Friend: A Source of Hope. The third friend is Thérèse of Lisieux, the saint I got to know while I was in the seminary. She's one of the most important people in my life because she saved my priestly vocation and gave me hope.

Now, I mentioned earlier that the book *True Devotion to Mary* had changed my life and given me hope in college because it claimed to offer the quickest and easiest way to become a saint. Well, shortly after entering the seminary, I began to feel that even the quickest and easiest path was not enough for me, which was a problem. I say that because I didn't want to become a priest unless I had at least some hope of becoming a saintly one. Well, I was losing that hope and felt tempted to give up.

About the time the temptations to leave the seminary were the worst, I started reading *Story of a Soul*, the spiritual autobiography of St. Thérèse of Lisieux. It changed my life, because Thérèse's spiritual doctrine (called "the Little Way") gave me hope that even someone like me could become a saint. The only problem was that I also ran into a lot of "thieves of hope" after reading it. That's the name I gave to the people I'd meet who would present Thérèse's teaching not as "the Little Way" for souls like me but as "the big way" for spiritual elites. For example, they'd say things like, "That little Thérèse isn't so little. She's actually quite big!" And then they'd go on to describe how heroic she was in her sacrifices, sufferings, virtues, and desires.

Hearing such things, I'd think to myself, "Maybe the Little Way is too big for me," and I'd get depressed. But then I'd go back to Thérèse's writings and find hope again … and then I'd listen to the thieves of hope again. So, my spiritual life became something of a roller coaster — high with hope one minute and down with discouragement the next.

Alright, so when it came time for me to write my licentiate thesis (a big research paper for a degree in theology that most people have never heard of), I decided to take it as an opportunity to get off the roller coaster. In other words, I diligently searched through nearly all of St. Thérèse's writings in order to discover once and for all whether or not the Little Way really could give hope of becoming a saint even to someone like me.

So what did I find? I found hope. Great hope. I discovered hidden treasures in Thérèse's teaching that made me say over and over, "Why haven't I heard this before?!" I read things that totally demolished the arguments of the thieves of hope, and those discoveries completely changed my life. To use Thérèse's own words, her teaching set me "full sail upon the waves of confidence and love."[1]

With this book, I now want to share those amazing treasures that gave me hope in the seminary and inspire me still. But before we begin, let me first connect the various dots that have come up as I've introduced you to my three friends.

Connecting the Dots

A Consecration to Divine Mercy — St. Thérèse-style. After my friend Mark called and told me that my next book needed to be on the Offering to Merciful Love, I knew what I had to do: Eat some humble pie. In other words, I had to go speak with my friend Fr. Chris and ask him if I could write the book on a Divine Mercy consecration after all. Thankfully, he was overjoyed to hear of my change of heart and enthusiastically gave me the green light.

So, this book truly is a consecration to Divine Mercy — *but in the style of St. Thérèse of Lisieux.* Specifically, it follows the theology of her Offering to Merciful Love, which is essentially a consecration to Divine Mercy. But before I get into what her Offering is all about, I should first say something about what a Divine Mercy consecration is.

Divine Mercy Consecration in General. The word "consecration" means to set apart for God. For instance, in the Church, the "consecrated life" refers to those who make vows of poverty, chastity, and obedience for the purpose of serving God according to the charism of a religious community. For example, a Carmelite nun (like St. Thérèse) makes religious vows so as to be set apart for God and to love and serve him through a life of contemplative prayer.

Of course, a personal consecration to Divine Mercy is not the same as making vows of poverty, chastity, and obedience. Rather, it's a self-offering to God (a setting of oneself apart for God) that anyone can make — whether the person is a member of the clergy, consecrated religious, or laity — and they do it for the specific purpose of *glorifying God's mercy.*

One of the best examples of a personal consecration to

Divine Mercy is actually a form of *Marian* consecration, a form that's taught by St. Maximilian Kolbe.

For Kolbe, Marian consecration means to offer oneself to God through Mary for the specific purpose of becoming *an instrument of mercy* in Mary's Immaculate hands as she is an instrument of mercy in God's hands.[2] In a sense, then, to make a Marian consecration according to the spirituality of St. Maximilian Kolbe — Marian consecration *Kolbe-style* — is already to make a consecration to Divine Mercy. In other words, it's a setting of oneself apart for God for the purpose of becoming an instrument of his mercy through Mary, the Mother of Mercy. But what I mean by the consecration to Divine Mercy "Thérèse-style" goes even deeper.

A St. Thérèse-style Consecration to Divine Mercy. Over the years, I've come across various devotional prayers labeled "A Consecration to Divine Mercy," and they've been great. But St. Thérèse of Lisieux, Doctor of the Church, has brought such devotional prayer to new and amazing heights. In fact, her consecration to Divine Mercy, what she calls her "Offering to Merciful Love," is really the culmination of her whole spiritual teaching on the Little Way, the crowning of her path to holiness, and, I'd even venture to say, *the most powerful form of consecration to Divine Mercy.*

While Week Three of the retreat will go into much more detail about St. Thérèse's Offering, here I'll just summarize its three most basic points.

First, Thérèse's Offering to Merciful Love is based on her profound insight into the love of the Heart of Jesus. Specifically, she recognized that Jesus' Heart is full of mercy and that he longs to pour out his Merciful Love, especially on sinners.

Second, she realized that sinners often close their hearts to the Lord's loving mercy, and their rejection of it causes Jesus great suffering.

Third, for the purpose of *consoling Jesus*, St. Thérèse asked the Lord to pour into her little soul all the rejected mercy that others don't want — and he gave it to her. *All of it*. And that experience set St. Thérèse happily on fire with Merciful Love.

Now, how the Lord gives this amazing gift of mercy, how we can receive it, and what all this means will be the topic of the retreat, which brings us to the next dot to connect.

A SEQUEL TO 33 DAYS TO MORNING GLORY. My old friend from college had said to me on the phone, "You need to do for the Offering to Merciful Love of St. Thérèse of Lisieux what you did for Marian consecration." Let me unpack that a bit.

Mark was referring to my book *33 Days to Morning Glory*, which is an updated and easy-to-use preparation for making a total consecration to Jesus through Mary. His point was basically that that book helped to make Marian consecration accessible to many more people. So, with that in mind, I knew exactly what he was getting at regarding the Offering to Merciful Love. Let me explain.

Sadly, the Offering to Merciful Love is one of the best-kept secrets in the Catholic Church. But I don't understand why. I mean, with the Offering, you have the culmination of the central teaching of the greatest and most popular saint of modern times — a Doctor of the Church, no less. Yet hardly anyone has ever even heard of her Offering to Merciful Love! I know this because in my travels, when I've given talks about the Offering, I've often begun by asking, "Who here has ever heard of the Offering to Merciful Love?" Truth be told, I've never seen more than about 5 percent of the people raise their hands.

So, I know what Mark meant. He knew that the Offering to Merciful Love is not well known. But he also knew that it's a big stick of spiritual dynamite and that someone just needs to light the fuse. In other words, he wants this amazing teaching to explode onto the Catholic scene and fill hearts with hope and holiness. In fact, he believes in its power to transform the world — and so do I.

I truly believe that this book can help light the fuse of the great grace-and-mercy bomb that is the Offering to Merciful Love — and I'm just the person to write it! What? I say that because I'm one of what St. Thérèse calls "the little souls." And one thing is clear in her teaching: God is pleased to use such souls as the special forces of his army. So, because I believe her teaching, I'm convinced that I can change the world — and that you can, too. Really. I'll make that point later in the retreat, but first, I should say some things about the connection between this book and *33 Days to Morning Glory.*

A Sequel That Stands Alone — But Shouldn't. You don't have to read *33 Days to Morning Glory* before reading this book — but I recommend you do. I say that because the essence of Marian consecration is to allow Mary to bring us to the pierced side of Jesus, which is the Fountain of Mercy. Okay, well, *33 Days to Morning Glory* is a book that prepares us to consecrate ourselves to Mary, so she can, in fact, bring us to that fountain.

This book, on the other hand, is about *drinking* from that fountain. And while we can get to the Fountain of Mercy without making a Marian consecration, such a consecration enables us to drink from it so much more deeply and easily. We'll learn the reasons for that during Week One of this retreat — which brings me to the structure of this book and how it works.

A Retreat That's Similar to Morning Glory. This book, like *33 Days to Morning Glory*, is a 33-day do-it-yourself retreat in preparation for consecration that's based on *heart-pondering prayer.* In other words, it doesn't focus on lots of vocal prayers each day of the retreat but, rather, on short spiritual readings that you can easily ponder in your heart throughout the day. So, you'll want to go over the daily reading each morning or the night before. That way, you can have the whole day to reflect on it. Of course, you should try not to miss a day of reading, but if you do, don't worry. Just make up the reading the next day.

As I already mentioned, this retreat lasts for 33 days, but the idea is not to begin on just any day. Rather, ideally, you should begin your preparation 33 days before an appropriate feast day. Of course, for a Marian consecration, such a day would be any Marian feast — and the same thing goes for a Divine Mercy consecration. I say that because, as we just learned, Mary leads us to Divine Mercy. But there are other days that have a special connection to Divine Mercy that would also be appropriate as consecration days. The most obvious one is the Second Sunday of Easter, Divine Mercy Sunday. A less obvious one is Trinity Sunday, which is the anniversary of when St. Thérèse first received her inspiration to offer herself to God's Merciful Love.

To help you figure out a good day to start your 33-day preparation for Divine Mercy consecration, check out the following chart with recommended feast days and their starting dates:

Start of the 33 Days	Feast Day	Consecration/Feast
January 9	Our Lady of Lourdes	February 11
February 20*	The Annunciation	March 25
Varies	Divine Mercy Sunday	Sunday after Easter
April 10	Our Lady of Fatima	May 13
April 28	The Visitation	May 31
Varies	Pentecost Sunday	50 days after Easter
Varies	Trinity Sunday	Sunday after Pentecost
Varies	Sacred Heart of Jesus	Friday after Corpus Christi
Varies	Immaculate Heart of Mary	Saturday after Corpus Christi
May 27	Sts. Peter and Paul	June 29
June 13	Our Lady of Mt. Carmel	July 16
June 19	St. Mary Magdalene	July 22
June 29	St. Alphonsus Liguori	August 1
July 12	St. Maximilian Kolbe	August 14
July 13	The Assumption	August 15
July 20	Queenship of Mary	August 22
August 3	St. Mother Teresa of Calcutta	September 5
August 6	Nativity of Mary	September 8
August 10	Holy Name of Mary	September 12
August 13	Our Lady of Sorrows	September 15
August 29	St. Thérèse of Lisieux	October 1
September 2	St. Faustina Kowalska	October 5

* During a leap year, when February has 29 days, the starting date is February 21.

September 4	Our Lady of the Rosary	October 7
September 13	St. Margaret Mary Alacoque	October 16
September 19	St. John Paul II	October 22
October 19	Presentation of Mary	November 21
November 5	Immaculate Conception	December 8
November 9	Our Lady of Guadalupe	December 12
November 22	Christmas	December 25
November 24	St. John the Apostle, Evangelist	December 27
November 29	Mother of God	January 1
December 23	Conversion of St. Paul	January 25
December 31	Presentation of the Lord	February 2

Of course, because the mystery of Divine Mercy touches all the mysteries of our faith and the life of every saint, you can certainly choose to consecrate yourself to Divine Mercy on any of the Church's solemnities, feasts, or memorials that are meaningful to you. Just remember to count back 33 days from the feast itself, with the day of consecration (the feast day) being the thirty-forth day.

What's Different from Morning Glory. Unlike *33 Days to Morning Glory*, this book does not include four weeks with four different saints. Rather, the various weeks will focus on one saint: Thérèse of Lisieux and her spiritual teaching. And that's okay because *St. Thérèse is the master*, the *Doctor of the Church* on these matters. Having said that, I will also include some of the teachings of St. Maria Faustina Kowalska, another great saint of mercy whose mission was closely related to that of St. Thérèse.[3]

While the focus of this retreat is Thérèse of Lisieux, we'll deal with different subject matter each week. So, for Week One, we'll focus on the backstory to Thérèse's teaching, a backstory that goes *way* back to the Garden of Eden, to the patriarch Abraham, and to Mary, the Mother of God. Week Two will then get into Thérèse's Little Way. Week Three will treat the Offering to Merciful Love. Then, Week Four will cover the topic of darkness as a bittersweet mystery in our own lives as well as in the life of St. Thérèse. Okay, but four weeks is only 28 days, so that leaves us with an extra five days. We'll use four of those five to review the main teachings of each week. Then, we'll use the last day to prepare ourselves to make the Offering to Merciful Love as a Divine Mercy consecration. Of course, before we can get to that last day, we'll need to start with the first, which now follows.

Week One
What Is Trust?

For St. Thérèse, it's all about trust. But what is trust? That's what we're going to ponder this week, using Sacred Scripture and its giants of trust. (By the way, I'm going to be using the words "trust" and "faith" pretty much interchangeably because in Thérèse's teaching, they're more or less the same.) Next week, we're going to start learning about St. Thérèse and her spiritual doctrine, which builds on this week's scriptural foundation.

DAY 1
Eve of Darkness[4]

We begin in the beginning with Eve and the fall of humanity, the Eve who reveals the opposite of trust, the Eve who caused the time of darkness.

Now, Eve's first mistake was that she listened to a liar — the Father of Lies. And what did he tell her? Of course, he told her a lie:

> [The serpent] said to the woman, "Did God say, 'You shall not eat of any tree of the garden'?" And the woman said to the serpent, "We may eat of the fruit of the trees of the garden; but God said, 'You shall not eat of the fruit of the tree which is in the midst of the garden, neither shall you touch it, lest you die.'" But the serpent said to the woman, *"You will not die. For God knows that when you eat of it your eyes will be opened, and you will be like God, knowing good and evil"* (Gen 3:1-5).[5]

"You will not die." The serpent boldly contradicts God's Word. For God had told Adam and Eve that if they ate from the forbidden tree they would die (see Gen 2:17). So, Satan, the Father of Lies, *makes God look like a liar.* And he goes on to make God look jealous, selfish, and conniving: "For God knows that when you eat of it your eyes will be opened, and you will be like God … ." In short, Satan casts doubt on God's goodness, making him look evil and untrustworthy.

We know the rest of the story. Eve disobeys God and leads Adam along the same path. But the key here is to notice how it all began: It began with a lie, a lie about God's Word, a lie that cast doubt on God's goodness and trustworthiness.

The *Catechism of the Catholic Church*, commenting on the first sin of Adam and Eve, gets to the heart of it all:

> Man, tempted by the devil, *let his trust in his Creator die in his heart* and, abusing his freedom, disobeyed God's command. This is what man's first sin consisted of. All subsequent sin would be disobedience toward God and *lack of trust in his goodness.*[6]

So, according to the *Catechism, it's all about trust.* More precisely, it's all about our *lack of trust.* To one degree or another, as sons and daughters of Adam and Eve, we all have a trust problem. We tend to distrust God. In other words, just as Adam and Eve *hid from God* when they heard him walking in the garden after their sin, so we, too, tend to hide from God, especially when our sins weigh heavily upon us. This is one of the effects of original sin, one of its "tragic consequences."[7] And so, what the *Catechism* says about Adam and Eve, to one degree or another, applies to us all: "They become afraid of the God of whom they have conceived a distorted image … ."[8]

And what has become distorted about our image of God? His goodness. We tend to doubt God's goodness. And when we don't fully believe that God is good, then we don't fully trust in him — and that's a problem. Why? Because, again, as the *Catechism* teaches, *all sin* involves a lack of trust in God's goodness.

To help heal our trust issues with God, on the initial day of this retreat, let's turn our attention to one of the great apostles of mercy for our time, a kindred soul to St. Thérèse: St. Maria Faustina Kowalska. Let's "visit" this humble nun and listen to her advice, as one of her own religious sisters once did:

> On the initial day of the retreat, I was visited by one of the sisters who had come to make her perpetual vows. She confided to me that she had no trust in God and became discouraged at every little thing. I

> answered her, "It is well that you have told me this, Sister; I will pray for you." And I spoke a few words to her about how much distrust hurts the Lord Jesus, especially distrust on the part of a chosen soul. She told me that, beginning with her perpetual vows, she would practice trust. Now I know that even [some] souls that are chosen and well advanced in the religious life or the spiritual life do not have the courage to entrust themselves completely to God. And this is so because few souls know the unfathomable mercy of God and His great goodness.[9]

Today's Prayer:

Come, Holy Spirit, fire of mercy.

Help me better to know the great and unsurpassable goodness of God.

DAY 2
Our Father in Faith

Yesterday, we learned that it's all about trust. More precisely, we learned that it's all about our *lack of trust* and that the wound of original sin causes us to tend to hide from God because we doubt his goodness. But there's something else about trust — a key ingredient that will help us better understand what it is, an ingredient that comes from our father in faith, our father in trust: the patriarch Abraham.

We all know the story. God put Abraham to the test. He commanded him to sacrifice his dearly beloved son, Isaac. And Abraham was willing to do it. He was willing to prove to God that he loved him more than his own son. And so the test was really all about love, right?

Wrong. It was actually all about *faith*, not love. Abraham's test was, above all, a test of faith. How so? Let me explain.

Abraham's whole walk with God was a walk of faith. For instance, God had called Abraham (who was then named Abram) from his home country: "Go from your country and your kindred and your father's house to the land that I will show you. And I will make of you a great nation, and I will bless you, and make your name great, so that you will be a blessing" (Gen 12:1-2). Abram believed God's Word, and off he went.

One night, after embarking on his journey, Abram complained to the Lord that he was childless and had no heir. God then directed his gaze to the multitude of stars in the sky and promised him, "So shall your descendants be" (Gen 15:5). Abram believed the Lord's Word, and he was later given a son through his wife, Sarah, though she was beyond childbearing years (see Gen 21:1-3). God promised Abram, who was now Abraham, that through that son, Isaac, he would establish an everlasting covenant with him and his descendants, blessing them with his saving presence and protection (see Gen 17:1-21).

Finally, in Genesis 22, God put Abraham's faith to the ultimate test when he commanded Abraham to sacrifice Isaac. This was the ultimate test of faith because it was *through Isaac* that God had promised to make Abraham blessed and a great nation. But here God was calling on Abraham to sacrifice Isaac! How could the world be blessed through a dead son? How could Isaac have children if he were killed as a child? Abraham's temptation clearly would have been to think that God is a liar, that he doesn't keep his promises. After all, to kill young Isaac would be to destroy the hope of the promised future blessing *through Isaac.*

What a hard test! Yet Abraham was ready to go through with it. He was ready to kill Isaac, as he had been commanded. Why? Because of his faith. The Letter to the Hebrews expresses it best:

> By faith Abraham, when he was tested, offered up Isaac, and he who had received the promises was ready to offer up his only-begotten son, of whom it was said, "Through Isaac shall your descendants be named." He considered that God was able to raise men even from the dead (Heb 11:17-19).

There is the marvel of Abraham's faith. He believed God's promise, even to the extent of "hoping against hope" (Rom

4:18) and considered that *God was able to raise up Isaac even from the dead.* That is faith. That is why Abraham truly is our father in faith. In fact, he teaches us the essence of faith, which is to believe God's Word, to believe that God is faithful to his promises, to believe that God is faithful even if it seems impossible.

Now, as our father in faith, Abraham is the complete opposite of our mother in doubt: Eve. After all, unlike Eve, Abraham refused to give in to the temptation to think that God is a liar, to think that God doesn't keep his promises, to think that God is not good. May Abraham's example of faith help us to overcome the effects of original sin caused by Eve's doubt. In other words, may it help us to trust God's promises and even to hope against hope.

Today's Prayer:

Come, Holy Spirit, fire of mercy.
Please give me such trust in God's Word
that I might even hope against hope.

DAY 3

Our Mother in Faith

Yesterday, we learned that Abraham is our father in faith — but there's a "greater than Abraham" here. Of course, I'm talking about Mary, our *mother* in faith. After all, she's the greatest example of faith, its "perfect embodiment,"[10] and its "purest realization."[11] And while Jesus, as true God, is the *object* of our faith (the one we believe in), Mary is the supreme *model* of faith (the one who best shows us what it means to believe in God).

So, what about Mary's faith? What does she show us about believing in God? Well, let me begin to answer that by first telling you an amazing secret: According to St. John Paul II, there's "*a kind of 'key'* which unlocks for us the innermost reality of Mary."[12] Imagine that. According to the greatest pope of the 20th century, there's a secret that reveals the mystery of Mary! Alright, so do you want to know what it is? Let me explain.

The great key, the great secret, has to do with Mary's *faith*, because faith gets to her deepest reality. And while we find this key in words spoken about Mary at the time of the Visitation, the words themselves refer back to her response to the angel at *the Annunciation*. Let's begin by reviewing that scene:

> In the sixth month the angel Gabriel was sent from God to a city of Galilee named Nazareth, to a virgin betrothed to a man whose name was Joseph, of the house of David; and the virgin's name was Mary. And he came to her and said, "Hail, full of grace, the Lord is with you!" But she was greatly troubled at the saying, and considered in her mind what sort of greeting this might be. And the angel said to her, "Do not be afraid, Mary, for you have found favor with God. And behold, you will conceive in your womb and bear a son, and you shall call his name Jesus. He will be great, and will be called the Son of the Most High; and the Lord God will give him the throne of his father David, and he will reign over the house of Jacob for ever; and of his kingdom there will be no end." And Mary said to the angel, "How can this be, since I have no husband?" And the angel said to her, "The Holy Spirit will come upon you, and the power of the Most High will overshadow you; therefore the child to be born will be called holy, the Son of God. And behold, your kinswoman Elizabeth in her old age has also conceived a son; and this is the sixth month with her who was called barren. For with God nothing will be impossible." And Mary said, "Behold, I am the handmaid of the Lord; let it be to me according to your word." And the angel departed from her (Lk 1:26-38).

Of course, we know the rest of the story. After the angel departs, Mary goes in haste to visit her cousin, St. Elizabeth (the Visitation), and when Elizabeth hears Mary's greeting, the child in her womb leaps for joy. But then, *Elizabeth gives the whole world a key to Mary's innermost reality.* "Filled with the Holy Spirit" and "with a loud cry," she proclaims two blessings, the last of which is the great key. Here it is: "*Blessed is she who believed that what was spoken to her by the Lord would be fulfilled*" (Lk 1:45).[13]

Now, according to St. John Paul II, that final blessing has a "fundamental importance."[14] Why? Because its words reveal the secret of Mary's faith, which is this: She believed that what the Lord had spoken to her at the Annunciation would be fulfilled. And so, her faith is like that of Abraham, as John Paul points out:

> Just as Abraham "*in hope believed against hope*, that he should become the father of many nations" (Rom 4:18), so Mary, at the Annunciation, having professed her virginity ("How shall this be, since I have no husband?") *believed* that through the power of the Most High, by the power of the Holy Spirit, she would become the Mother of God's Son in accordance with the angel's revelation: "The child to be born will be called holy, the Son of God" (Lk 1:35).[15]

So, if we want to understand the mystery of Mary, we should reflect on the fact that she believed God's Word, even when it seemed impossible. She hoped against hope, believing that, as the angel said, "with God nothing will be impossible."

Today's Prayer:

Come, Holy Spirit, fire of mercy.
Help me to believe that with God
nothing will be impossible.

DAY 4
Mary's Pilgrimage of Faith

Yesterday, we learned that there's a key to Mary's innermost reality, a key to understanding her faith — the blessing of Elizabeth: "Blessed is she who believed that what was spoken to her by the Lord would be fulfilled." Now, while those words firstly refer to the Annunciation and the moment when Mary believed the angel's words that she would be the mother of the Son of God, they also refer to her whole life of faith — or, as St. John Paul II puts it, her "pilgrimage of faith."

Now, contrary to overly pious belief, Mary didn't constantly have angels waiting on her at her home in Nazareth, helping with the housework and changing Jesus' diapers. Nor did she hear about the Child Jesus going around town changing water into apple juice and multiplying cookies. Rather, the Holy Family of Jesus, Mary, and Joseph had an ordinary life of work, recreation, and prayer. In other words, Mary (and her husband, Joseph) walked by faith and not by sight, as St. John Paul II makes clear:

> During the years of Jesus' hidden life in the house at Nazareth, *Mary's life too is "hid with Christ in God"* (cf. Col 3:3) through faith ... [She] is in contact with the truth about her Son only in faith and through faith! She is therefore blessed, because "she has believed," and continues to *believe day after day* ... during the years of the hidden life at Nazareth.[16]

So, the hidden life of the Holy Family — all that time from Jesus' childhood and adolescence that we hear almost nothing about in Sacred Scripture — was not only hidden from us but, in a certain sense, was hidden from Mary, too! I mean, she lived her "contact with the truth about her Son" *in the darkness of faith*, a faith that was "linked with a sort of 'night of faith.'"[17] In other words, her pilgrimage of faith came with "*a particular heaviness of heart*,"[18] because it had to be lived under "a kind of 'veil,'"[19] a veil that prevented Mary (and Joseph) from fully grasping that mystery in the midst of which they daily lived (see Lk 2:48-50). And so, the Pope concludes:

> [T]hus even his Mother, to whom had been revealed most completely the mystery of his divine sonship, lived in intimacy with this mystery only through faith! Living side by side with her Son under the same roof, and faithfully persevering "in her union with her Son," she "*advanced in her pilgrimage of faith*" ... And so it was during Christ's public life too (cf. Mk 3:21-35) that day by day there was fulfilled in her the blessing uttered by Elizabeth at the Visitation: "Blessed is she who believed."[20]

Alright, but what was it that Mary believed *specifically* as she lived "under the same roof" with Jesus and during his public life? Of course, we know that at the Annunciation she believed God's Word, hoping against hope that she would become the mother of the Son of God through a virginal conception. But what else did she believe that merited a blessing? Well, her thinking may have gone something like this:

- Here is a great king! ... Yet he's wrapped in swaddling clothes and resting in a poor manger? *Yes, I believe.*
- Here is the Son of God! ... Yet he's silently nursing at my breast? *Yes, I believe.*
- Here is a king whose reign will last forever! ... Yet our rulers were just seeking to stone him? *Yes, I believe.*
- Yes, I believe everything that God promised about Jesus will be fulfilled, even if everything about him is a "sign of contradiction" (Lk 2:34).

Truly, day by day through the hidden life in Nazareth and during Jesus' public ministry, the blessing of Elizabeth was fulfilled in Mary. She remained steadfast in faith as she held on to the words spoken to her by the Lord and pondered them in her heart. But her pilgrimage of faith had not yet met its ultimate test. We'll hear about that terrible trial tomorrow.

Today's Prayer:

Come, Holy Spirit, fire of mercy.
Help me to believe in God and his love for me,
even when life seems meaningless, routine, and empty.

DAY 5

Mary's Trial of Faith

Just as Abraham's pilgrimage of faith met its ultimate test when he was called to sacrifice Isaac, so Mary's pilgrimage of faith met a similar test. However, while Abraham did not have to go through with the sacrifice, Mary had to watch and be present during the torture and slaughter of her dearly beloved Son all the way to its agonizing end. She had to stand and consent to the immolation of the victim.[21] She had to remain there in faith, hoping against hope.

It was there on Calvary, there at the foot of the Cross, that we find in Mary the glorious perfection of faith. It was there, in the midst of the most terrible darkness, that we paradoxically see the luminous blessing of Elizabeth shine forth with ever-greater glory: "Blessed is she who believed that what was spoken to her by the Lord would be fulfilled!" Yes, blessed is she who believed at the foot of the Cross. Blessed is she who believed in the impossible. Blessed is she who believed "that God was able to raise men even from the dead" (Heb 11:19). That is faith. Again, that is the glorious perfection of faith. That is the greatest light of faith, which shines amid the deepest darkness.

Now, ponder once again the words of the angel that Our Lady believed regarding her Son, Jesus:

> He will be great ... and the Lord God will give him the throne of his father David, and he will reign over the house of Jacob for ever; and of his kingdom there will be no end (Lk 1:32-33).

And now, reflect on St. John Paul II's reaction to and commentary on those words in view of Mary's ultimate trial of faith:

> [S]tanding at the foot of the Cross, Mary is the witness, humanly speaking, of the complete *negation of these words.* On the wood of the Cross her Son hangs in agony as one condemned. "He was despised and rejected by men; a man of sorrows ... he was despised, and we esteemed him not": as one destroyed (cf. Is 53:3-5). How great, how heroic then is the *obedience of faith* shown by Mary in the face of God's "unsearchable judgments"! How completely she "abandons herself to God" without reserve, "offering the full assent of the intellect and the will" to him whose "ways are inscrutable" (cf. Rom 11:33)! And how powerful too is the action of grace in her soul, how all-pervading is the influence of the Holy Spirit and of his light and power![22]

Wow. That's a lot of exclamation marks from a pope. Three in a row! Why all the enthusiasm? It's because, again, we've arrived at the perfection of faith. We've arrived at the moment when we see "how great, how heroic" is Mary's faith, the moment when we see "how completely she 'abandons herself to God' without reserve." We've arrived at the moment when Elizabeth's words of blessing, as John Paul puts it, "seem to re-echo with supreme eloquence, and the power contained within them becomes something penetrating."[23] And it's probably becoming clear now as to why that blessing *penetrates.*

It penetrates because *we need that blessing.*

All of us will go through times when our faith is severely tested. We'll experience times of excruciating darkness and even agony, and we'll wonder, "Where is God?" We'll not understand his ways. We'll feel as if all is lost, that God no longer loves us, that he has abandoned us. And then we'll remember — I hope we'll remember — Mary's example of faith at the foot of the Cross. We'll recall that she, too, did not fully understand. She, too, stood in darkness. She, too, had a heart that was bleeding and broken. We'll also remember that she didn't give in to the darkness, that she clung to God with the light of faith.

And then — I hope — we'll remember *the blessing*. We'll remember Elizabeth's words: "Blessed is she who believed that what was spoken to her by the Lord would be fulfilled." And I hope that "the power contained within [that blessing] will become something penetrating" *for us*. In other words, I hope we'll see how Elizabeth's blessing can apply *to us*, that the following words can be spoken *to us*: "Blessed are *you* who believed that what was spoken *to you* by the Lord would be fulfilled."

And what was spoken to us? What's the word of the Lord *for us*? It's the word of the Cross. It's the word of love spoken through Christ's death on the Cross, the word of love that Mary intimately shared in on Calvary. It's the word from Scripture: "Greater love has no man than this, that a man lay down his life for his friends" (Jn 15:13). It's the truth that God loves us, that God loves *you*, no matter what. I hope that by holding on in faith to that greatest expression of love in the midst of our own trials and darkness, we'll find peace, and even joy — and maybe even sing a song of praise.

We'll talk about Mary's song of faith and praise tomorrow.

Today's Prayer:

Come, Holy Spirit, fire of mercy.
Help me to believe in God and his love for me,
even when the darkness surrounds me.

DAY 6
Mary's Song of Faith

Yesterday was a bit heavy and dark. But today is a day for rejoicing! Today is a day for us to realize that faith (trust) leads to joy — great joy — and to songs of praise.

Now, recall that Mary, after she believed in the word spoken to her by the angel, went to visit her cousin, St. Elizabeth. And by now, how could we forget the blessing? "Blessed is she who believed that what was spoken to her by the Lord would be fulfilled." And what was Mary's immediate response? She sang a song of praise, her famous Magnificat, that glorious proclamation of God's mercy, which begins:

> My soul proclaims the greatness of the Lord,
> My spirit rejoices in God my Savior,
> For he has looked with favor on his lowly servant (Lk 1:46-48).

So, after her trust in the Lord's words was blessed, Mary immediately praised the Lord. *And such praise itself is a powerful act of trust, pleasing to the Lord.*

Alright, well, now it's time for a personal story.

When I first learned this great lesson — that praise itself is a powerful act of trust — it had a profound effect on my life. While I already shared how it happened in the book *Consoling the Heart of Jesus*, I think it's worth repeating this week as we ponder the question, "What is trust?" and on this day, specifically, as we reflect on "Mary's Song of Faith."

First, I learned the connection between praise and trust during a pilgrimage to the National Shrine of The Divine Mercy in Stockbridge, Massachusetts, when I was a seminarian. The precise moment came during a conversation with Fr. Seraphim Michalenko, MIC, an expert on the message of Divine Mercy that comes to us through St. Faustina:

> I asked Fr. Seraphim, "Father, it's all about consoling the Heart of Jesus, isn't it?"[24]
>
> He looked pleased with my question and answered with an enthusiastic, "Yes, it is!"
>
> Encouraged by his response, I continued, "And we want to console Jesus in the best possible way, right?"
>
> "Right," he said.
>
> "And the best way to console him is to remove the thorn that hurts his Heart most, the thorn that is *lack of trust [in his Merciful Love].*"
>
> "Right again."
>
> Confidently, I stated my conclusion, "And so

the best way to remove that thorn and console him is to *trust* him."

"Michael, you're absolutely right."

"Great!" I said to myself, "It's all about trusting Jesus in order to console him."

At that point, I thought I was all set. I thought I completely understood. Well, that's when Fr. Seraphim interrupted my contentment: "And how do you *live* trust? What's its concrete expression in your daily living?"

I was stumped. "I don't know."

His answer changed my life: *"The way you live trust is by praise and thanksgiving, to praise and thank God in all things. That's what the Lord said to St. Faustina."*

As soon as I heard Fr. Seraphim's words, I knew he was right, because I remembered how St. Mother Teresa of Calcutta had often written about the importance of accepting everything with a smile, with praise and thanksgiving. I also thought to myself, "Yes, this is true. For this is the Little Way of surrender, acceptance, and childlike trust taught by St. Thérèse of Lisieux." Specifically, I think I had in mind one of my favorite passages from her autobiography:

> Jesus does not demand great actions from us but simply surrender and gratitude. Has he not said: "OFFER TO GOD THE SACRIFICES OF PRAISE AND THANKSGIVING"[?] (Ps 49:14).[25]

We'll learn more about St. Thérèse's Little Way next week. But for now, today, let's console Jesus and live out our trust in God's mercy by making a sacrifice of praise and thanksgiving with Mary.

Today's Prayer:

Come, Holy Spirit, fire of mercy.

Fill my heart with a faith-filled song of praise and thanksgiving to God for his tender love and mercy!

DAY 7

New Eve of Light and Life

This week, we've been looking at the meaning of trust, the heart of which comes through the examples of Abraham and Mary, who were blessed because they believed that what God had promised them would be fulfilled. But while Mary far surpasses Abraham as an example of faith, she also provides something that Abraham cannot: the grace to believe, the grace to trust. Let me explain this crucial point.

Faith is a gift of grace. It's no human work. So how do we obtain it? We obtain it through Mary. Why do I say that? Because Mary is the New Eve.[26]

As we learned on Day 1, the old Eve brought about the wound of original sin, a wound that causes us to have a distorted image of God, a wound that causes us to doubt God's goodness, a wound that causes us to tend to hide from God. The wound, then, is clearly about God. And so God uses another woman, a New Eve, to help heal the wound that the old Eve caused — a New Eve, a "woman," who was announced from the beginning, a woman who would be at enmity with Satan, a woman whose offspring would crush the serpent's head (see Gen 3:15).

In a certain sense, God needs this woman's help. Why? Because, again, *the wound has to do with God.* So God has two problems: (1) He wants us fallen creatures to believe in his Word and to trust in his goodness, but that's something he can't force, because trust, like love, must be given in freedom. (2) Due to the wound of original sin, we already tend to distrust God, so when he draws close to us, we often run and hide.

You might say, then, that the New Eve is God's secret weapon *because our wound doesn't have to do with her.* After all, she's a creature like us. And best of all, she's a kind and gentle mother — and who can be afraid of such a mother?

So Mary can win hearts in a way that even Jesus Christ can't. What? Well, I say that because Jesus is God, and again, our wound has to do with God. That's why even today, after all he has done for us, people still avoid Jesus. But a mother, who is not God, can often win over such straying hearts. And what does our heavenly mother do when she wins such hearts? *She brings them to Jesus.* That's Mary's whole passion and purpose. She just wants to heal the wound. She just wants us to believe in God and trust in his mercy. She just wants us to come to understand God's goodness and accept his Merciful Love. And she's effective — not only because she's such a tender mother, but also because, as the Church teaches, she's a Mediatrix of grace.[27]

By a "Mediatrix of grace," I don't mean that Mary is the source of grace. The Heart of Christ, pierced with a lance and overflowing with blood and water — *that* is the source of grace. But Mary *leads us* and *brings us* to that source of grace, the Fountain of Mercy. Also, she herself helps open our hearts to receive that mercy. Why? Because of what she went through on Calvary.

On Calvary, Mary's Heart was pierced with a sword, as Simeon had foretold (see Lk 2:35). But her pierced Heart is different from that of her Son's. Again, when his Sacred Heart was pierced, it became the Fountain of Mercy, the source of mercy. But when Mary's Immaculate Heart was pierced, it became an *instrument of grace* that *opens hearts* to receive God's mercy (see Lk 2:35). Now, of course, the piercing of her Heart hurt. In fact, it was the unfathomable suffering of her motherly Heart at Calvary that makes her Heart an instrument of grace, a Mediatrix of grace.[28] And it's her suffering, more than that of any other creature, *that makes up for what is lacking in the suffering of Christ.*

What? Is something lacking in Christ's suffering? According to St. Paul, there is. He says, "In my flesh, I complete what is lacking in the sufferings of Christ" (Col 1:24). Now, of course, in one sense, there's *nothing* lacking in Christ's suffering. In fact, his suffering and death on the Cross obtained the grace of salvation for everyone who has ever lived, is living, and will live, even to the end of time. In other words, the love that flows from the Lord's pierced Heart is an *infinite ocean of mercy.* Problem is, *not everyone accepts, receives, and draws from such a superabundant source.* They close their hearts to Christ's saving love. So really, the "lack" is on the side of sinful humanity — *but we can help make up for that.*

Through our suffering, lovingly united with Christ's, we can obtain for people the grace to accept his gift of salvation. For instance, I can pray and sacrifice for you, and it makes a difference. You can pray and sacrifice for me, and it makes a difference. But no human being makes more of a difference than Mary when it comes to helping people obtain the grace and mercy flowing from the Heart of Jesus. Why? Again, because Mary is the New Eve.

Mary truly is the New Eve who brings us to the New Adam on the new tree of life, the Cross. And once there, she lovingly encourages us not to eat forbidden fruit but to drink from the blessed fountain of eternal life, the Fountain of Mercy. And through the grace of her suffering at the foot of the Cross, our gentle mother opens our hearts to receive the gift of salvation that comes to us in the love and mercy that flows from Christ's pierced side. Such saving faith truly is a gift of Christ through Mary. And such a gift leads the Church to rightly declare, "Death through Eve, life through Mary."[29]

Today's Prayer:

Come, Holy Spirit, fire of mercy.
Bring me, through Mary, to the Fountain of Mercy.

WEEK TWO
The Little Way

Last week, we covered the biblical foundation of St. Thérèse's teaching on trust, which, as we'll learn this week, is called "the Little Way." This Little Way will bear striking similarities to Abraham's and Mary's faith, the essence of which is to believe that what is spoken by the Lord will be fulfilled. In fact, this young woman from the French town of Lisieux, who died in 1897, well before her twenty-fifth birthday, and who lived a quiet, sheltered childhood among doting sisters and then a quiet, sheltered adolescence as a cloistered Carmelite nun (with some of those very same sisters) — that *woman, after Abraham and Mary,*[30] *is perhaps the Church's greatest example of the faith that "hopes against hope." Thus, St. Thérèse truly merits both blessings of Elizabeth: "Blessed is she who believed that what was spoken to her by the Lord would be fulfilled" and "Blessed are you among women"— of course, we'd have to add, "after Mary."*

But how can this be? How can such a seemingly unimportant woman be so amazingly blessed? It can be so because God's ways are not our ways, and he delights in lifting up the lowly and making the greatest from the littlest — and perhaps no sinner is more lowly and little than Thérèse of Lisieux.

DAY 8
None More Lowly

I just said that perhaps no one among sinful humanity is more lowly and little than Thérèse of Lisieux. Of course, that may be hard to believe. After all, St. Pius X called her "the greatest saint of modern times,"[31] and in 1997, she became one of only 33 Doctors of the Church.[32] So, sure, God lifts up the lowly. But is she really *that* lowly?

Well, consider the following.

First, Thérèse Martin grew up in a France that was deeply affected by the Jansenist heresy, a heresy that teaches a joyless moral rigorism, emphasizing fear and justice, punishment and severity, judgment and condemnation. It proclaims not the Good News of God's mercy for sinners but its own bad news of God's consuming wrath for whoever dares to commit the slightest infraction against what it sees as his many oppressive rules.

It teaches that few are saved, that you have to be perfect to go to Jesus, and that you must earn his love, especially by multiplying great works and painful sacrifices.

Now, Thérèse was deeply affected by Jansenism during her younger years. Perhaps its influence came through her mother, Zélie, whose own mother was severely Jansenistic and used to hound her poor daughter with the litany, "That's a sin, that's a sin, that's a sin."[33] But leaving aside the question of exactly how Thérèse fell under Jansenism's influence, we can say this much: It affected her at a very young age. For instance, as a child, whenever she'd make some mistake or do something wrong, even without meaning to, she'd be filled with anxiety[34] and ask for "pardons which never end."[35] Her mother relates, "We tell her she's forgiven but in vain. She goes on crying just the same."[36]

We see Jansenism's effect on Thérèse in her later childhood as well. For instance, in preparation for her First Holy Communion at age 10, she made and recorded 1,949 small sacrifices and 2,773 short prayers![37] (Thankfully, Jesus himself later taught her, as she put it, "not to count up my acts."[38]) Much worse, though, was her painful bout with scruples, which often goes along with Jansenist thinking.

Thérèse's battle with scruples began during her retreat in preparation for her First Holy Communion, a retreat that was led by a very severe priest. She remembers the experience as follows: "What [the priest] told us was frightening. He spoke about mortal sin, and he described a soul in the state of sin *and how much God hated it.*"[39]

Thankfully, Thérèse could confide in her dear sister Marie whenever she was tempted to think that God had rejected her — but Marie's words only brought temporary comfort, and Thérèse's scruples followed her even into the Carmelite convent (also called "Carmel"). In fact, her sister Pauline (Mother Agnes) wrote: "The fear of offending God 'poisoned' Thérèse's existence at the beginning of her religious life."[40]

Jansenism poisoned Thérèse's early religious life not only by creating in her an excessive fear of offending God but also by causing her to develop an unhealthy preoccupation with suffering. This becomes clear through her letters of the time. For instance, and this is just one example among many, we read:

> Holiness does not consist in saying pretty things, not even in thinking or feeling them! ... It consists in *suffering* and suffering from *everything* ... Holiness! One must conquer it at sword point, one must suffer ... one must agonize ... .[41]

Now, apart from the influence of Jansenism, Thérèse's lowliness is also the result of her simply being a very fragile and broken little girl. Having lost her biological mother to cancer at the age of 3 and her adopted mother to Carmel at the age of 9, she became an emotional mess who would cry at the slightest provocation. In fact, others used to say to her, "You cry so much during your childhood, you'll no longer have tears to shed later on!"[42] (Her oversensitivity wouldn't be healed until she received the grace of her "Christmas conversion" at the age of 14.[43])

Because of Thérèse's deep emotional fragility — which led to a debilitating psychological breakdown at age 10[44] — her sisters sheltered her and doted on her so much that she became a socially awkward outcast and loner when she finally started going to school. In fact, the other school kids bullied her and made fun of this girl who didn't know how to join in their games and couldn't even comb her own hair.[45]

In the midst of her extreme loneliness and sensitivity, Thérèse deeply longed to be loved. In fact, hers was so great a longing that, she admitted, given the opportunity, she basically would have thrown herself into the arms of the first creature who came along. As she herself put it, "With a heart such as mine, I would have allowed myself to be taken and my wings to be clipped ... I know that without Him, I could have fallen as low as St. Mary Magdalene."[46] Thanks be to God, the Lord showed amazing mercy on this littlest of souls by actually preserving her ahead of time from a life of grave sin *by removing the obstacles* that would have caused her to fall.[47]

Now, Thérèse was painfully aware of all the weakness just described and more — so don't even try to tell her that she's not a little soul! Were you to say that, she'd probably look you in the eye and respond in all seriousness, "My friend, *there's none more lowly than I.*"

Today's Prayer:

Come, Holy Spirit, fire of mercy.
Help me to recognize my own lowliness
and to rejoice in God's mercy.

DAY 9

Discovery of the Little Way

Yesterday, we learned that Thérèse Martin was a little soul, indeed. Still, from the time of her youth, she had *bold* desires: She wanted to become a saint, and not just any saint, but a *great* saint. A story from her childhood helps us understand this — a story she calls "a summary of my whole life."[48]

One day, Thérèse's older sister Leonie had decided she'd outgrown some of her playthings. So she offered to her little sisters, Céline and Thérèse, a basket full of such items. Céline chose one item that pleased her. But when it came to Thérèse's turn, the future saint suddenly exclaimed, "I choose all!" and proceeded to take the entire basket.

That story expresses well how Thérèse approached the spiritual life and the path to sanctity in particular. She understood that "there were many degrees of perfection" and she wanted the *highest degree*, saying to the Lord, "My God, *I choose all!* … '*I choose all*' that You will!"[49]

Later, Thérèse would express her bold desires for holiness in an even more audacious way, saying that she wanted to love God *even more than Teresa of Avila*, the great Carmelite Doctor of the Church![50] However, she also realized her weakness and littleness. And so, for Thérèse, saints like the great Teresa of Avila were like *eagles*, soaring on the heights of holiness; whereas, she simply saw herself as a weak little bird without strength and unable to fly. In fact, she readily admitted, "I am not an eagle." Nevertheless, she went on to explain, "but I have … an eagle's EYES AND HEART." Then, she continued, "[So,] in spite of my extreme littleness I still dare to gaze upon [the Lord], and my heart feels within it all the aspirations of an *Eagle*."[51]

Such is the boldness that led Thérèse to discover the Little Way. Rather, it's more accurate to say that the Lord couldn't help but *reveal* it to her: "Because I was little and weak He lowered Himself to me, and He instructed me secretly in the *things* of His *love*."[52] In the following passage, she sets up this joyful revelation of "the things of His love":

> I have always wanted to be a saint. Alas! I have always noticed that when I compared myself to the saints, there is between them and me the same difference that exists between a mountain whose summit is lost in the clouds and the obscure grain of sand trampled underfoot by passers-by. Instead of becoming discouraged, I said to myself: God cannot inspire unrealizable desires. I can, then, in spite of my littleness, aspire to holiness. It is impossible for me to grow up, and so I must bear with myself such as I am with all my imperfections. *But I want to seek out a means of going to heaven by a little way, a way that is very straight, very short, and totally new.*[53]

So, the little bird with the heart of the eagle, the little bird who is well aware of her weaknesses, is also totally confident that God could not have given her the heart of an eagle *without also providing her the means of realizing her desires.* Therefore, there must be such a path! There must be a path for little souls like her: a "straight," "short," and "totally new" way. Well, Thérèse is a great Doctor of the Church because she discovered such a way — rather, she *rediscovered* it. Yes, she rediscovered the very heart of the Gospel, the Good News that God lifts up the lowly:

> We are living now in an age of inventions, and we no longer have to take the trouble of climbing stairs, for, in the homes of the rich, an elevator has replaced these very successfully. I wanted to find an elevator which would raise me to Jesus, for I am too small to

> climb the rough stairway of perfection. I searched, then, in the Scriptures for some sign of this elevator, the object of my desires, and I read these words coming from the mouth of Eternal Wisdom: "*Whoever is a LITTLE ONE, let him come to me.*" And so I succeeded. I felt I had found what I was looking for. ... The elevator which must raise me to heaven is Your arms, O Jesus! And for this I had no need to grow up, but rather I had to remain *little* and become this more and more.[54]

Question: When you read the lives of the saints, do they seem like eagles soaring on the heights while you're just a little bird that can't fly? In other words, do they seem like towering mountains while you're just a small grain of sand? If so, *then you're a little one.* You're one who recognizes your poverty, weakness, brokenness, and sin. And now, Thérèse has just announced to you the good news that there's a new invention, a "spiritual elevator," that provides a way to the heights for little souls. It's a way that's "very 'straight' because it's entirely vertical, very 'short' because it avoids the spirals of the staircase,"[55] and "totally new"— or at least it feels that way because it rediscovers the heart of the Gospel, namely, God's mercy for the little and the lowly. We'll learn more about that part tomorrow.

Today's Prayer:

Come, Holy Spirit, fire of mercy.
Give me the heart of an eagle,
a burning longing to choose all that you will for me.

DAY 10

Discovery of Divine Mercy

Thérèse's discovery of the Little Way — a "straight," "short," and "totally new" way to the heights of holiness for little souls — is really a discovery of *Divine Mercy.* In other words, it's a rediscovery of the very heart of the Gospel. And what's the heart of the Gospel? The *Catechism* says it's "the revelation in Jesus

Christ of *God's mercy* to sinners."[56] Now, in Thérèse's day, which was during the terrible time of Jansenism, this truly would have seemed like a "totally new" and joyful revelation. Indeed, amid the foul and stuffy Jansenist atmosphere, Thérèse's discovery of the Little Way came as a breath of fresh air, leading her to pray, "O my God, You surpassed all my expectation. *I want only to sing of Your mercies.*"[57] Yes, singing is in order — for in rediscovering the Gospel, Thérèse had also rediscovered the joy of the Gospel.

And what is the Gospel? Again, it's the Good News of God's mercy for sinners. It's the Good News that Jesus didn't come for the righteous but for sinners. It's the Good News that Jesus has the Heart of the Good Shepherd who will even leave behind the 99 to go in search of the one lost sheep. It's the Good News that God doesn't love us because *we're* so good but because *he's* so good, that he loves us not because we deserve it but because *we desperately need it.* It's the Good News that God's love is like water, which always goes to the lowest place. It's the Good News that God's ways are not our ways, that God isn't attracted to our gifts, virtues, and talents, but rather, to our weakness, brokenness, and sin. And this is the very definition of mercy, which the parable of the Good Samaritan seems to reveal most clearly:

> A man was going down from Jerusalem to Jericho, and he fell among robbers, who stripped him and beat him, and departed, leaving him half dead. Now by chance a priest was going down that road; and when he saw him he passed by on the other side. So likewise a Levite, when he came to the place and saw him, passed by on the other side. But a Samaritan, as he journeyed, came to where he was; and when he saw him, he had compassion, and went to him and bound up his wounds, pouring on oil and wine; then he set him on his own beast and brought him to an inn, and took care of him. And the next day he took out two denarii and gave them to the innkeeper, saying, "Take

> care of him; and whatever more you spend, I will repay you when I come back" (Lk 10:30-35).

The Good Samaritan, as it says later, is "the one who showed mercy" (v. 37). So, what is mercy? More specifically, what is Divine Mercy? Well, it's when God doesn't pass us like the priest and Levite but, rather, like the Samaritan, comes to us where we are, sees our weakness, brokenness, and misery, and then acts to heal us and bring us to a place of comfort and rest. In other words, mercy involves two things: the *heart* and the *arms.* It's God's *being moved to compassion* at seeing our suffering (heart) and then taking *action* to help alleviate it (arms). And that's really what's going on with the Little Way and its famous elevator.

The Little Way is about the *compassion* of Jesus (heart), who sees the suffering of little souls who long to attain the heights of holiness but who are too little to climb the "rough stairway of perfection." It's about the *action* of Jesus (arms), who reaches down out of pity and picks up trusting little souls to place them on the heights.

So, the elevator is *the mercy of Jesus.* It's the mercy of Jesus in action, the compassion of Jesus reaching out to lift up the lowly. And all this, again, gets back to the heart of Sacred Scripture, which is saturated with mercy. Saint Thérèse herself points this out in a remarkable passage at the end of her autobiography, a passage that weaves together her favorite truths of the Gospel — the truths that she has rediscovered:[58]

> I have only to cast a glance in the Gospels and immediately I breathe in the perfumes of Jesus' life, and I know on which side to run. I don't hasten to the first place but to the last; rather than advance like the Pharisee, I repeat, filled with confidence, the publican's humble prayer. Most of all I imitate the conduct of Magdalene; her astonishing or rather her loving audacity which charms the Heart of Jesus also attracts my own. Yes, I feel it; even though I had on my conscience all the sins that can be committed, I

> would go, my heart broken with sorrow, and throw myself into Jesus' arms, for I know how much He loves the prodigal child who returns to Him.[59]

Are you beginning to "breathe in the perfume" of Jesus' mercy, which is the very heart of the Gospel? Are you beginning to love Thérèse's way of humble confidence in Divine Mercy? If you still haven't begun to savor its sweetness, ponder Thérèse's advice to her sister Céline, which brings us back to the Heart of the Good Shepherd: "[D]o not fear, the poorer you are the more Jesus will love you. He will go far, very far, in search of you, if at times you wander off a little."[60] Or, as Jesus himself put it to St. Faustina: "The greater the sinner, the greater the right he has to My mercy."[61]

Today's Prayer:

Come, Holy Spirit, fire of mercy.
Unveil for me the mystery at the heart of the Gospel,
the mystery of the Heart of Christ:
his tender mercy for sinners.

DAY 11
Do Three Things

As we learned yesterday, the Little Way is all about the heart of the Gospel: Divine Mercy. It's all about remaining little and then arriving at the heights of holiness through the descending mercy of Jesus.

Alright, so we simply remain "little" and then wait for the Lord to stoop down, take us into his arms, and raise us to the heights, right? Well, lest we mistakenly think we just need to kick back, eat ice cream, and wait for our canonizations, St. Thérèse shares with us an illuminating metaphor of a little child at the bottom of a staircase (probably the "rough stairway of perfection").

Now, the child, who is all of us little souls, cannot even climb the first step of that big staircase — we're too little. But Thérèse tells us to *try*. She says, "Raise your little foot to scale the stairway of holiness."[62] Of course, we won't be successful, but Thérèse then adds, "God requires you only to demonstrate your good will." In other words, we just need to give it a try. And as we do, Thérèse tells us that God will be "conquered by [our] futile efforts" and will then descend the stairway, gather us into his arms, and take us to the heights.[63]

So, Thérèse's point seems to be that our efforts in the spiritual life are absolutely necessary but also *absolutely useless.* What? I mean that in the sense that St. Mother Teresa of Calcutta meant when she'd often say, "God does not call us to be successful but to be faithful." In other words, applied to our spiritual lives, the Lord doesn't demand that we *attain* all the virtues (success) but that we simply *keep trying* (faithfulness). For those on the Little Way, the success part isn't what's most important. In fact, in a sense, it's sometimes better that little souls *aren't* successful.

Here's what I mean: Jesus likes to keep little souls little. After all, if they were suddenly to see themselves bounding up the rough stairway of perfection with great strides, it might go to their heads, and they'd be too "big" for Jesus to lift. And so, the Lord sometimes permits that little souls remain in the darkness of certain vices or sins so they won't fall into worse ones, like the sin of pride. But don't just take my word for it. Listen to what Thérèse herself said to one of her novices who often failed in the practice of virtue:

> And if the good God wants you weak and helpless like a child ... do you believe that you will have less merit? ... Agree to stumble at every step therefore, even to fall, to carry your cross weakly, to love your helplessness. Your soul will draw more profit from it than if, carried by grace, you would accomplish with enthusiasm heroic actions that would fill your soul with personal satisfaction and pride.[64]

In sum, then, the Little Way is often a little way of *darkness.* It's about accepting that we are to put up with ourselves — with all the darkness of our weakness, brokenness, and sin — without getting discouraged. It's recognizing, without giving up, that some struggles are *chronic*. It's realizing, without despairing, that they may be with us till our dying day. But it's also about realizing that this does *not* prevent us from becoming saints.[65]

So, even if we have to go to Confession over and over for the same sins, we shouldn't get discouraged. And we should listen to Pope Francis, who said, "The Lord never tires of forgiving, never! It is we who tire of asking his forgiveness."[66] Of course, we need to be sorry for our sins and make a firm purpose of amendment. But if we do that, if we keep *trying*, then there's no end to the Lord's mercy, and we can believe that he can and *will* satisfy our desires for holiness.

Tomorrow, we'll learn more about how God can and will bring little souls to the heights of holiness. For now, let's just consider that if we want to live the Little Way, we must do three things: (1) *Recognize the darkness:* Recognize the darkness of our littleness and brokenness. (2) *Keep trying:* Keep trying to grow in holiness and do little things with great love. (3) *Keep trusting:* Keep trusting and believing that God will satisfy our desires for holiness, even if we don't yet fully understand how.

Today's Prayer:

Come, Holy Spirit, fire of mercy.

Help me to do three things: (1) recognize the darkness of my littleness, (2) keep trying to grow in holiness, and (3) keep trusting in your mercy.

DAY 12
You Will Become a Saint

If you truly live the Little Way — if you recognize the darkness of your littleness, keep trying to grow in holiness, and trust in the Lord's promise of mercy — *then you will become a saint.* It's that simple. And if you're very little and your trust is great, then you may even become a *great* saint. What?

Before we get to that, here's something that may be even more shocking: As St. Thérèse was dying, because she believed what she taught, because she believed that she would be a great saint, she herself collected the clippings of her nails and invited her sister Pauline (Mother Agnes) to take them, presumably to be used as relics![67] Also, she encouraged the other sisters to keep the rose petals that had touched her crucifix, saying, "They will help you perform favors later on; don't lose one of them."[68] *What?* Did the mortal sickness that devoured Thérèse's poor lungs also affect her brain? No. Thérèse was completely sane, and her words are actually consistent with the doctrine of her Little Way.

It's like this. According to traditional Catholic spiritual wisdom, to think you will be a great saint is basically to disqualify yourself from becoming one. After all, to think such a thing (not to mention collecting relics of yourself) is certainly pride, right? Well, not in Thérèse's case. The reason has to do with her revolutionary approach to two virtues: magnanimity and humility.

The word "magnanimity" comes from the Latin words *magnus*, meaning "great," and *animus*, meaning "soul." So, it's a kind of "great-souled-ness" that moves a person to *aim high* in the spiritual life. For instance, it was because of her extraordinary magnanimity that St. Thérèse once said, "I would so much like to love [God] ... to love Him more than He has ever been loved."[69] And such magnanimity is a good thing.

Still, having said that, traditional Catholic spiritual wisdom teaches that the virtue of *humility* is supposed to keep magnanimity in check. It's supposed to pull back great desires for holiness, like reining in a horse. For instance, the virtue of humility would respond to Thérèse's magnanimous statement about wanting to love God more than he's ever been loved before with something like this:

> Come on. Don't say *that*. Be a little more humble and realistic. I mean, look at who you are. Frankly, you're a very broken little girl. So why not just aim to be a little saint who simply makes it into heaven without spending time in purgatory? Isn't that enough for you, given how weak and little you are? Why don't you just leave great holiness to the great souls?

That's certainly reasonable, but Thérèse would have none of it. She didn't believe that humility's role is to rein in the horses of her great desires for holiness. On the contrary, she saw humility as being what smacks magnanimity's horses in the rear, sending them racing to the moon! In other words, it's not *in spite* of humility but, rather, *because* of humility that she believed she could become one of the greatest of saints. And this firm belief stemmed from her insight into God's amazing mercy.

Remember that God's Merciful Love is like water: It rushes to the lowest place — and Thérèse knew this. Therefore, she saw her humility, that is, her awareness of her littleness, as her greatest treasure.[70] Why? Because she knew it was her littleness that attracted God's Merciful Love. And because she was so little and trusted completely in Divine Mercy, she believed that God's mercy would surely rush to the lowest place — her little soul! — and fill it to overflowing.

Wonderful. Good for St. Thérèse. But what does all this have to do with becoming a great saint? Well, … *everything*. Why? Because *what is holiness but the Merciful Love of God poured into our hearts*? (See Rom 5:5.) For Thérèse, *that* is the true and greatest holiness. Moreover, such holiness is not a human work but, rather, God's work, a work of Divine Mercy rushing down to the lowest place. And because Thérèse believed she was the littlest soul, she, therefore, believed she could become one of the *greatest* of saints. In fact, she even told the Lord, "[H]ere on earth, I cannot conceive of a greater immensity of love than the one which it has pleased You to give to me freely, *without any merit of my part*."[71] Actually, come to think of it, she did have one "merit": her trust. After all, it's trust that opens the floodgates of God's mercy, allowing it to come rushing down, down, down into little souls.[72]

What a revolution in Catholic spiritual theology! Thérèse believed that she was the weakest and littlest of souls (humility) and *therefore* she felt confident of becoming one of the greatest of saints (magnanimity). So, her humility didn't rein in her desires for holiness. Rather, it sent them racing to the heights. Better yet, it brought her down low, *deep down low* into a hollow abyss that a superabundance of Divine Mercy could rush down into. That is literally the deepest holiness! And it's not pride to hope for it.[73] Rather, it's humility. And such hope is what Thérèse wants every little soul to experience:

> O Jesus! why can't I tell all little souls how unspeakable is Your condescension? I feel that if You found a soul weaker and littler than mine, which is impossible, You would be pleased to grant it still greater favors, provided it abandoned itself with total confidence to Your Infinite Mercy ... I beg You to cast Your Divine Glance upon a great number of little souls. I beg You to choose a legion of *little* Victims worthy of Your LOVE![74]

So, in view of Thérèse's prayer for little souls, I repeat: If you live the Little Way, that is, if you recognize the darkness of your littleness, keep trying to grow in holiness, and trust in the Lord's promise of mercy, *you will become a saint.* It's that simple. And if you're very little and your trust is great, you may even become a *great* saint, like St. Thérèse — just please don't keep your nail clippings.

Today's Prayer:

Come, Holy Spirit, fire of mercy.
Though weak, broken, and sinful,
help me to trust that I can become a great saint
through the amazing power of Divine Mercy.

DAY 13
Prophet of Mercy

Yesterday, we learned that Thérèse of Lisieux is a spiritual genius for the way she revolutionized at least one aspect of Catholic spiritual theology. Specifically, she taught us that, because of Divine Mercy, we can become great saints not in spite of our littleness but, rather, because of it! But more than a spiritual genius — which she certainly is — *St. Thérèse is a prophet.* Let me explain.

In the Church today, there's a lot of talk of the "time of mercy," a time of great grace and blessing. Why? Simply put, it's because the times are so evil. In other words, as we learn from Sacred Scripture, in times of great evil, God gives *even greater grace*: "Where sin increased, grace abounded all the more" (Rom 5:20).

Now, that's great. But even with such a solid scriptural foundation, we can't simply decide for ourselves that it's a "time of mercy." Such a decision would need to come from God, and someone with authority would have to announce it. Well, Pope Francis has such authority, and he did announce it. Here's what he said:

> [L]isten to the voice of the Spirit that speaks to the whole Church in this our time, which is, in fact, the time of mercy. I am certain of this ... It is the time of mercy in the whole Church. It was instituted by [St.] John Paul II. He had the "intuition" that this was the time of mercy ... It was explicit in [the year] 2000, but it was something that had been maturing in [John Paul's] heart for some time. He had this intuition in his prayer ... It is a consignment that he gave us, but which comes from on High.[75]

So, we're in a time of mercy, and we have that on the authority of the Pope. Of course, while it's been passed on to us by the Pope, it's also a gift that "comes from on High," a gift that comes from God himself.

Now, what if, as a special gift for the time of mercy, God wanted to make it easier than ever before to become a saint? What if he wanted to give us a special gift of holiness in our day? Of course, he could give such a gift if he wanted to. He's God. *But is he giving such a gift?* That's the key question. And to answer it, God himself would have to let us know by choosing someone with authority to announce it to us. Well, that's where St. Thérèse comes in *as a prophet.*

According to then-Cardinal Joseph Ratzinger (later Pope Benedict XVI), "[A] prophet is someone *who tells the truth on the strength of his contact with God* — the truth for *today* … ."[76] Now, St. Thérèse of Lisieux is such a prophet. As a Doctor of the Church, she teaches us a truth for today with authority, and that truth is this: God wants to work some of his greatest miracles of mercy in the whole history of the Church *today*. In other words, *right now*, he wants to take some of the littlest of souls and make them into some of the greatest of saints.[77]

Of course, we covered some of the spiritual mechanics of how he might do this in our reflections of the last two days. But here, I want us to better appreciate what we learned over those days by putting it in the context of a *prophetic announcement* for the present time of mercy in the Church. More specifically, I want us to see our present preparation for making an Offering to Merciful Love not as an exercise in learning spiritual theology but, rather, as a response to God's gift of mercy in this time of mercy. I want us to see our preparation to consecrate ourselves to Divine Mercy as a way of letting God work a great miracle of mercy in us and for our time.

Why is such a context important? It's important because when we see that our consecration preparation is part of a gift "from on High" *for our time*, it carries more weight. It helps us appreciate that, by consecrating ourselves to Divine Mercy, we're letting ourselves be carried into a greater work of the Spirit that's going on right now, in our day. Moreover, it puts the focus where it belongs, namely, *on trusting God*.

Let me put it this way. Why couldn't Jesus work many miracles in his hometown of Nazareth? (See Mk 6:5.) Remember that? All he could do was small miracles, like maybe healing somebody's ingrown toenail. But why couldn't he work the big ones? It was because of *people's lack of faith*. Think of it! The all-powerful God-man, the one who walks on water, casts out demons, and heals the deaf and the blind — *that* great man, in a certain sense, is *powerless* when we don't give him our faith! But it's faith, it's *trust*, that unleashes the power of his mercy. That's why St. Thérèse so emphasized trust. That's why Jesus asked St. Faustina to paint an image of Divine Mercy with the signature, "Jesus, I trust in you."[78] It's because in this present time of mercy, Jesus wants to work the great miracle of forming the littlest of souls into the greatest of saints. But he needs our trust to do it.[79] So, will we give it to him?

Today's Prayer:

Come, Holy Spirit, fire of mercy.
Teach me to pray with my whole heart,
"Jesus, I trust in you."

DAY 14

No More 'Thieves of Hope'

Yesterday, we learned that St. Thérèse of Lisieux is a prophet. Specifically, we learned that she's a prophet of mercy who announces God's desire in the present time of mercy to work the amazing miracle of mercy of forming us into great saints through the Little Way. But for him to work this miracle, we need to give him our trust: "Jesus, I trust in you." But maybe there's something holding us back. Maybe we can't yet fully give him our trust — I know I couldn't.

I shared in the introduction that when I first learned about the Little Way, it filled me with hope that maybe even someone like me could become a saint. But I also shared that I'd then run into "thieves of hope." Remember them? They're the people who would say things like, "That St. Thérèse wasn't so little. She was actually quite big." And then they'd go on about Thérèse's impressive virtues, desires, sacrifices, and sufferings such that I'd think to myself: "Well, maybe the Little Way is too big for me. Maybe it's just the big way wrapped in a sugar-coated crust and a flowery rhetoric." And with that, I'd get discouraged. But then, eventually, I'd read something in Thérèse's writings that would give me hope. And *then*, it wouldn't take long before the thieves of hope were getting me discouraged again. (This went on and on.)

Tired of being on such a roller coaster of spiritual ups and downs, I decided to read just about everything St. Thérèse ever wrote, trying to find out if the Little Way really could help someone like me to become a saint. Well, my research was not in vain. I found what I was looking for. Rather anticlimactically, it's called "Letter 197" in Thérèse's collected letters, and it offers some of the most consoling words I've ever read. It destroys all the arguments of the thieves of hope and set me "full sail upon the waves of confidence and love."[80] But before I share it, I should first give a bit of background.

Letter 197 is St. Thérèse's response to a letter from her sister Marie (Sr. Marie of the Sacred Heart), which itself was a response to one of Thérèse's teachings that we read earlier: the little bird that could not fly. Remember that image? (We covered it in the reading for Day 9.) Well, that story of the pitiful little bird with the heart of an eagle was actually Thérèse's attempt to explain her Little Way to her sister Marie.

Problem is, Marie didn't like the story. She felt it was inaccurate. After all, she lived in the same convent as Thérèse. So, every day, she saw her sister's impressive desires, sacrifices, and sufferings right up close, and she concluded that the future saint was no little bird at all. Instead, she was an eagle! Moreover, Marie felt that she herself was the little bird and that there was no hope for her to love God as Thérèse loved him.

Even though she writes like one of the thieves of hope, I thank God for Marie. I mean, I couldn't have put the objection better myself. (Actually, I did put it myself because I just paraphrased her thoughts, but you get the idea.) Anyway, Thérèse responds to Marie with her glorious Letter 197. The letter speaks for itself, so let it speak to you. Please read it slowly and prayerfully:

> Dear Sister, ... How can you ask me if it is possible for you to love God as I love Him?
>
> ... If you had understood the story of my little bird, you would not have asked me this question. My [_______ (fill in the blank: virtues, talents, many gifts, etc.)] *are nothing*; they are not what give me the unlimited confidence that I feel in my heart. They are, to tell the truth, the spiritual riches that *render one unjust*, when one rests in them with complacence and

when one believes they are *something great* ... Ah! I really feel that it is not this at all that pleases God in my little soul; what pleases Him is *that He sees me loving my littleness and my poverty, the blind hope that I have in His mercy* ... That is my only treasure ... [W]hy would this treasure not be yours?

Oh, dear Sister, I beg you, understand your little girl, understand that to love Jesus, to be His *victim of love*, the weaker one is, without desires or virtues, the more suited one is for the workings of this consuming and transforming Love ... [B]ut we must consent to remain always poor and without strength, and this is the difficulty ... Ah! let us remain then *very far* from all that sparkles, let us love our littleness, let us love to feel nothing, then we shall be poor in spirit, and Jesus will come to look for us [and] He will transform us in flames of love.

... Oh! how I would like to be able to make you understand what I feel! ... It is confidence and nothing but confidence that must lead us to Love.[81]

Today's Prayer:

Come, Holy Spirit, fire of mercy.

Help me to embrace the Little Way with all my heart.

Week Three

The Offering to Merciful Love

Nine months after St. Thérèse discovered her Little Way, something happened that catapulted her far along its path. It was June 9, 1895 — Trinity Sunday. During Mass, the young nun received the inspiration and burning desire to offer herself to Merciful Love. Immediately afterward, she went to her sister Pauline (Mother Agnes), who was prioress at the time, and asked permission to make the Offering. Mother Agnes recalled the occasion during an interview: "When she asked me this, her face was all lit up, as if she were on fire with love. I let her do it."[82] *Next, when asked if Thérèse had made the Offering just once and forgotten about it, Mother Agnes replied, "Oh, no, never; she constantly repeated it, and her whole life revolved around it. On her deathbed she said to me one day: 'I often repeat my act of consecration.'"*[83]

What is this Offering to Merciful Love, this "consecration" to Divine Mercy around which Thérèse's "whole life revolved"? That's what we're going to explore this week.

DAY 15

What It's Not

Probably the best way to begin to understand the Offering to Merciful Love is to contrast it with what *it's not*.

Recall that in the France of Thérèse's day, the heresy of Jansenism had a deep influence on Catholic spirituality. Well, Thérèse's own Lisieux convent certainly felt its effects. That's largely because of a popular and terribly rigorist book on Carmelite spirituality called *The Treasure of Carmel*. Among other things, the book asserts that every Carmelite should offer herself as a victim soul to God's justice, and several nuns from the Lisieux convent did just that.[84] Alright, so what did that offering mean? Let me begin to answer by introducing you to Sr. Marie of Jesus, a Carmelite from Luçon, France.

Sister Marie died in the spring of 1895, and her obituary arrived at the Lisieux convent on June 8, where it was read aloud in the refectory, probably that same day.[85] The next day, June 9, Thérèse received the inspiration to make her Offering to Merciful Love. Did Sr. Marie's obituary have an influence on Thérèse? It seems that it did, and the reason should become clear as we proceed.

First, according to the obituary, Sr. Marie "very often offered herself as a *victim to divine Justice*."[86] (Thérèse would have duly noted those last words.) Second, it's clear from the obituary that Sr. Marie had fallen under the influence of Jansenism, as we can tell from some of her anxious last words: "I don't have enough merits, I must acquire more of them."[87] (Those words would have made an impression on the saint of the Little Way, who did not want to lay up merits for heaven but wanted to work for love alone.) Finally, the obituary also includes the following statement from Sr. Marie, which she uttered in the midst of her mortal agony: "I am bearing the harshness of divine Justice … divine Justice! … divine Justice!"[88]

So, what's going on here? Well, basically, to offer oneself as a victim soul to God's justice, as Sr. Marie did, is to make a sort of deal with the Lord, a deal that would go something like this: "Lord, please give to me all the punishment that's due to sinners, and then give to sinners the blessings I would normally receive as a faithful religious." Perhaps surprisingly, the Lord would take people up on such an offer. Specifically, like Sr. Marie of Jesus, they would often come down with some illness that would cause terrible suffering and an agonizing death.

Thérèse had often heard of such victim souls to God's justice, and she was deeply impressed with their generosity. Now, of course, the "little bird" with the "eyes and heart of an eagle" also wanted to be generous with the Lord. Nevertheless, probably with Sr. Marie in mind, she wrote the following:

> I was thinking about the souls who offer themselves as victims of God's Justice in order to turn away the punishments reserved to sinners, drawing them upon themselves. This offering seemed great and very generous to me, *but I was far from feeling attracted to making it.*[89]

After reading these lines, one can almost hear the sighs of relief from all little souls. Thankfully, Thérèse was very much attracted to *another* kind of offering: the Offering to Merciful Love. We'll look at what that is tomorrow. For now, we can reflect on the refreshing perspective from which the saint of Lisieux approached the idea of offering herself as a spiritual victim:

> *How GOOD is the Lord, his MERCY endures forever!* It seems to me that if all creatures had received the same graces I received, God would be feared by none but would be loved to the point of folly; and through *love*, not through fear, no one would ever consent to cause Him any pain. I understand, however, that all souls cannot be the same, that it is necessary there be different types in order to honor each of God's perfections in a particular way. To me He has granted His *infinite Mercy*, and *through it* I contemplate and adore the other divine perfections! All of these perfections appear to be resplendent *with love*; even His Justice (and perhaps this even more so than the others) seems to me clothed in *love*. What a sweet joy it is to think that God is *Just*, i.e., that He takes into account our weakness, that He is perfectly aware of our fragile nature. What should I fear then?[90]

Clearly, Thérèse's path is one of mercy and not justice. In fact, she even sees God's justice through the lens of mercy, a lens that transforms the "harshness of divine Justice," as Sr. Marie of Jesus had put it, into a justice that's "clothed in *love*." Moved by this merciful perspective, Thérèse comes up with a spiritual victimhood that's based on mercy not justice, on love and not fear, on tenderness and not severity. Indeed, her Offering is well suited for the little souls who long to attain the heights of holiness but who are too little to climb the rough stairway of perfection, too little to take the path of fear and harsh justice.

Thank God for St. Thérèse. Thank God that she discovered a way of spiritual victimhood that not only allows even little souls to be generous but also *sets them on fire with love*. We'll learn more about that tomorrow.

Today's Prayer:

Come, Holy Spirit, fire of mercy.
Fill me with Merciful Love so that, through it,
I may see all of God's perfections,
including his justice, as clothed in love.

DAY 16
What It Is

Yesterday, we learned that St. Thérèse's Little Way does not culminate in an offering to Divine Justice but, rather, in an offering to *Divine Mercy*. So, what is it? Thérèse herself tells us as she makes an ardent prayer to the Lord:

> O my God! Will Your Justice alone find souls willing to immolate themselves as victims? Does not Your *Merciful Love* need them too? On every side this love is unknown, rejected; those hearts upon whom You would lavish it turn to creatures, seeking happiness from them with their miserable affection; they do this instead of throwing themselves into Your arms and of accepting Your infinite *Love*. O my God! Is Your disdained Love going to remain closed up within Your Heart? It seems to me that if You were to find souls offering themselves as victims of holocaust to Your Love, You would consume them rapidly; it seems to me, too, that You would be happy not to hold back the waves of infinite tenderness within You. If Your Justice loves to release itself, this Justice *which extends only over the earth*, how much more does Your Merciful Love desire to *set souls on fire* since Your Mercy *reaches to the heavens*. O my Jesus, let me be this happy victim; consume Your holocaust with the fire of your Divine Love![91]

From this beautiful prayer, we begin to arrive at the essence of the Offering to Merciful Love. And the key lines that reveal its essence are actually two questions. The first one is this: "Does not Your *Merciful Love* need [victims] too?" The implied answer is *yes.* Jesus needs little souls to receive his Merciful Love. And that's the beauty of Thérèse's path. It's not a path on which Jesus gives grace and mercy because we deserve it but, rather, *because he feels the need to give it.*

Of course, we can walk the path of merit by focusing on what we "deserve." In other words, we can be anxious about our merits like the poor victim of justice, Sr. Marie of Jesus, who said from her deathbed, "I don't have enough merits, I must acquire more of them." Or we can travel the path of mercy by giving our attention to Jesus, who longs for souls into whom he can pour his Merciful Love.

One expert on Carmelite spirituality contrasted these two paths (that of merit and that of mercy) as follows: "[God] brings about [our sanctification] by the diffusion of grace which He gives according to our merits, *or simply to satisfy the need of his mercy.*"[92] I don't know about you, but I choose the latter path!

Okay, so here's the second key question in Thérèse's ardent prayer: "Is Your disdained Love going to remain closed up within Your Heart?" That is the million-dollar question! But it's not really a question for Jesus; it's a question *for us.* Actually, it's a question *for you.* (I've already shared what path I've chosen.) So, what about you? Are you going to have pity on Jesus? Are you going to console his Heart by letting him pour into your soul the love that others have rejected? If you say yes to this Offering, then it seems that Jesus would be "happy" not to "hold back" the waves of … what? Infinite justice? Infinite harshness? No. *Infinite tenderness.* Now, who wouldn't want *that*?

Alright, but before you answer which path you'll choose — justice or mercy, harshness or tenderness — I'd like to bring in the testimony of another great saint of Divine Mercy. I do this because it may be hard to believe that Jesus actually "needs" us and that we truly can give relief to his Sacred and Merciful Heart. To help us understand, listen to what the Lord himself said to St. Faustina about the rejected grace and mercy of his Heart:[93]

> I desire to bestow My graces upon souls, but they do not want to accept them. You, at least, come to Me

as often as possible and take these graces they do not want to accept. In this way *you will console My Heart.* Oh, how indifferent are souls to so much goodness, to so many proofs of love! My Heart drinks only of the ingratitude and forgetfulness of souls living in the world. They have time for everything, but they have no time to come to Me for graces.[94]

... The flames of mercy are burning Me. I desire to pour them out upon human souls. Oh, what pain they cause Me when they do not want to accept them![95] ... I am looking for souls who would like to receive My grace.[96]

So, do you want to "console" Jesus by receiving his grace? Will you accept the rejected mercy that burns his Heart? Will you be, as St. Thérèse put it, his "happy victim" by letting him pour into your soul his "waves of infinite tenderness"? Will you offer yourself as a victim soul to his Merciful Love?

Maybe you're not quite ready. Maybe you're saying to yourself, "That sounds wonderful, but *what's the catch?*" In other words, "What's it going to cost me?" Great question. We'll answer it tomorrow.

Today's Prayer:

Come, Holy Spirit, fire of mercy.
Prepare my heart to receive waves of infinite tenderness from the Heart of Jesus.

DAY 17

What's the Catch?

The Offering to Merciful Love sounds great: For the purpose of consoling Jesus, we would ask for and accept all the rejected love and tender mercy that other souls don't want. Wonderful. But what's the catch? Clearly there's a catch when it comes to making an offering to Divine Justice: *lots of suffering!* (Remember Sr. Marie of Jesus? Yikes!) So what's the catch when it comes to making an offering to Merciful Love? Well, there is, indeed, a catch — but it's not a scary one. Let me explain.

We're just outside the walls of Jerusalem at Calvary, and Jesus is dying on the Cross. Do you see him there, all bloody, bruised, and broken? He's a victim soul to *Divine Justice.*[97] After all, Jesus made a kind of deal with the Father. He basically said, "Father, please give to me all the punishment due to sinners, and give to sinners all the blessings of my own divine Sonship." That's really what's taking place there on the Cross: Jesus is paying the price of sin and bearing the harsh burden of Divine Justice so we don't have to and so we might enjoy the gift of salvation. The "catch" for him, as a victim to Divine Justice, is the terrible pain of his Passion, culminating in his three-hour-long agony on the Cross.

Now, Mary is also there on Calvary, standing at the foot of the Cross. Her presence there helps us to understand the "catch" that comes with being a victim soul to *Merciful Love.* I say that because, while she was not physically crucified at Calvary, she did suffer a kind of spiritual crucifixion. How? Well, let me put it this way: I'm sure any mother who has had to watch her child suffer through an agonizing illness will tell you she immediately would have switched places with her child if given the opportunity. Okay, so with that in mind, now reflect on the idea that Mary probably has more motherly love in her Immaculate Heart than all other mothers combined. Not only that, but her Son is the most lovable child of all. Not only *that*, but Mary had to watch her child go through a suffering worse than anyone has ever had to bear.

Okay, so all that should give us a sense of Mary's suffering as she stood at the foot of the Cross. But, when we think of it, that suffering isn't so scary — at least it's not as repulsive as the idea of a violent, bloody, and torturous death. Why not? Because Mary's suffering at Cavalry was the suffering of *compassion.*

Now, compassion means "to suffer with," and such suffering, by its very nature, is other-directed. In other words, the focus is on another person, not on ourselves. And when our focus is not on ourselves when we're suffering, although our pain is certainly real, we often don't even notice it. We're too focused on the beloved who suffers. On the other hand, when we stub our toe or have a terrible headache, it's hard not to focus on ourselves, and then we really notice the pain. So, in a sense, compassionate suffering is easier to bear and less scary than physical suffering. It's also something that gets to the heart of who we're called to be.

As Christians, our hearts are supposed to be merciful. In other words, we're supposed to be moved with compassion at the suffering of others. Unfortunately, our sins, the sins of others, and the pains of life are very good at hardening our hearts, which makes us less compassionate, less merciful, and less like Jesus.

Well, the Offering to Merciful Love is all about helping us grow in compassion, and it begins with *having compassion for Jesus.* It begins with seeing that he longs to pour his Merciful Love out on sinners and that so many reject his love. Then, for the purpose of consoling Jesus, we ask for all that rejected mercy. And what happens next? Jesus gives it. His tender mercy comes rushing into our hardened hearts, purifying them and, thereby, making them more compassionate, loving, and sensitive.

So, that's the catch! To offer ourselves to Merciful Love is to let our hearts be more deeply moved by the suffering of others. It's to allow our hearts to become more like the heart of St. Francis of Assisi, who, in his great compassion for Jesus, went around weeping and crying out loud, "Love is not loved! Love is not loved!" It's to allow our hearts to become more like the heart of St. Mother Teresa of Calcutta, who attentively listened to Jesus' painful cry from the Cross: "I thirst!"[98] It's to allow our hearts to be healed of indifference toward the pain and suffering of our neighbor. In short, it's to allow Jesus to make our hearts more like his.

Now, don't worry. The heart-healing graces of the Offering to Merciful Love don't usually come all at once. I mean, Jesus tends to *gradually* heal our hearts as we live the Offering. But it does involve real pain. After all, compassion for those who suffer wounds the heart. But it's a beautiful wound — the wound of love! Thérèse's sister Céline (Sr. Geneviève of the Holy Face) puts it best:

> We must not confuse [my sister's desire to be a victim to Merciful Love] with the … victims of justice. Thérèse's heart was wounded, it is true, but here, love was answered by love … the wound of love! Indeed, there is nothing that is sweeter, nor more terrible.[99]

So, the Offering to Merciful Love not only consoles the Heart of Jesus, but it also (paradoxically) heals our hearts by wounding them with love. The Offering, thereby, makes life both "sweet" and "terrible" (in a good way!) as our hearts awaken in compassion to the reality of Christ's Mystical Body (the Church) suffering in both its Head and members. But if all that isn't enough to convince us to choose to make the Offering to Merciful Love, then maybe this will: If we make and live the Offering, we need not fear purgatory. *What?* More on that tomorrow.

Today's Prayer:

Come, Holy Spirit, fire of mercy.
Make my heart like the tender Heart of Jesus,
full of mercy and compassion.

DAY 18
No Purgatory?

Yesterday, we learned that the Offering to Merciful Love heals our hardened hearts, making them more sensitive and compassionate. One result of that heightened sensitivity is a deeper feeling of longing for God. And guess what: That's a lot like purgatory. Really. Saint Faustina once had a vision of purgatory (that place of suffering for the souls of those who die in a state of grace but who are still in need of purification[100]), and she asked the souls there what their greatest suffering was. They all replied in unison, "*[L]onging for God.*"[101]

Alright, so does the Offering to Merciful Love make this life into purgatory? Well, in a certain sense, *yes*, because it increases our longing for God. But don't worry. In this life, it's a sweet longing and a particularly good thing. It's especially good because it not only opens our hearts to deeper prayer and can make life more joyful, but it also keeps us from having to go to the real purgatory in the next life. In fact, St. Thérèse believed that for little souls who live the Little Way and make the Offering to Merciful Love, *purgatory can easily be avoided*. And by that, I certainly *don't mean* it's easy to avoid because it's easy to go to hell! Rather, I mean it's easy to bypass purgatory and go *straight to heaven*, like the saints do. Let's let Thérèse herself explain this amazing point.

The saint of the Little Way believed that after she made her Offering to Merciful Love, she no longer needed to fear purgatory. She describes the reason to her sister Pauline (Mother Agnes), who had given her permission to make the Offering:

> You permitted me, dear Mother, to offer myself in this way to God, and you know the rivers or rather the oceans of graces that flooded my soul. Ah! since the happy day, it seems to me that Love penetrates and surrounds me, that at each moment this *Merciful Love* renews me, purifying my soul and leaving no trace of sin within it, and I need have no fear of pur-

> gatory. I know that of myself I would not merit even to enter that place of expiation since only holy souls can have entrance there, but I also know that the Fire of Love is more sanctifying than is the fire of purgatory. I know that Jesus cannot desire useless sufferings for us, and that He would not inspire the longings I feel unless He wanted to grant them.[102]

Does this sound like someone who regrets having offered herself to Merciful Love? Of course not. And, in fact, the line that follows this paragraph makes it even clearer: "Oh! how sweet is the way of Love!" Yes, it's sweet because *love is sweet*, and it's also more effective at making us holy: "[T]he Fire of Love is more sanctifying than is the fire of purgatory." In fact, for Thérèse, love is "the chief plenary indulgence"[103] that can keep us from purgatory. Moreover, she explains, "God who is all gentleness would moderate to excess the temporal punishment due to sin, because of our love."[104]

So, love carries us along the way, making everything, in a certain sense, *easy*.[105] It's the way our loving and merciful God intended for us. But when we get too "big" — in other words, when we don't fully and confidently abandon ourselves to God in this life — then we have to endure "useless sufferings," we have to endure "the fire of purgatory." But Thérèse wants us to avoid it, and she believes that God wants us to avoid it, too.

Actually, according to Thérèse, God doesn't just want us to bypass purgatory; he wants us to stop talking about it as if it were nearly impossible to avoid. In fact, she believed that such talk hurts the Lord. For instance, after hearing some of the other nuns talking about how they'd probably end up in purgatory, Thérèse responded, "Oh! How you grieve me! You do a great injury to God in believing you're going to purgatory. When we love, we can't go there."[106] And as for one of her novices who told her, "I fear purgatory,"[107] Thérèse had this to say:

> You do not have enough trust. You have too much fear before the good God. I can assure you that He is grieved over this. You should not fear purgatory

> because of the suffering there, but should instead ask that you not deserve to go there in order to please God, Who so reluctantly imposes this punishment. As soon as you try to please Him in everything and have an unshakable trust He purifies you every moment in His love and He lets no sin remain. And then you can be sure that you will not have to go to purgatory.[108]

How can we be sure that we "will not have to go to purgatory"? Thérèse's advice is something we've already heard: *Keep trying* ("As soon as you *try* to please Him in everything … "). And she also said something else that's familiar: *Keep trusting* (" … and have an unshakable trust"). So, when we keep trying and keep trusting, God "purifies [us] every moment in His love and He lets no sin remain."

Okay, so that covers two of our "three things" for living the Little Way that we learned on Day 11: Keep trying and keep trusting. But where's the third thing? Where's the call to "*recognize the darkness* of our littleness"? We find that part of Thérèse's teaching in her response to one of her novices, Sr. Marie of the Trinity, who was concerned about her chances of avoiding purgatory.

Sr. Marie had asked St. Thérèse, "If I fail even in the small things, may I still hope to get straight to heaven?" Now, Thérèse knew the young nun's weaknesses very well, and yet she still responded with beautiful words for little souls: "Yes! God is so good. He will know how He can come and get you. But despite this, try to be faithful, so that He does not have to wait in vain for your love."[109] Yes, God is so good to little souls who recognize their weakness. So, let's try to be faithful, and let's trust in God's promise of mercy.

Today's Prayer:

Come, Holy Spirit, fire of mercy.
Help me to live my life
so I'll go straight to heaven when I die.

DAY 19
Three Objections

At this point, we've learned what the Offering to Merciful Love is *not* (an offering to Divine Justice), what it *is* (an act of mercy toward Jesus), what it *costs* (our hardness of heart), and what it *frees us from* (the fires of purgatory). Now, before we begin looking at the text of the Offering itself (tomorrow), I'd like to cover three potential objections to it.

The first objection has to do with yesterday's reflection on purgatory. Now, some of us may have read it and thought that perhaps Thérèse is encouraging the sin of presumption by telling us to believe that we can bypass purgatory. Well, she actually would be if she were telling us we can expect to go straight to heaven without sorrow for our sins and without making a firm purpose of amendment. But that's not what she teaches. In fact, her emphasis on *trying* includes fostering a sorrow for one's sins and making a firm resolution not to sin again.

So, if we object, then maybe we're simply looking for justice. Maybe we think Thérèse is being too indulgent. Maybe we want people to have to pay more for their sins. Well, in that case, we'd just be disagreeing with Thérèse and siding with Sr. Fébronie.

Sister Marie Fébronie, the 67-year-old subprioress at Thérèse's convent, had heard about the 19-year-old novice mistress' teaching on purgatory. She didn't like it because she thought it was presumptuous and too lenient — so, she confronted Thérèse about it. In response, with love and kindness, the young nun calmly tried to explain the matter, but Sr. Fébronie would have none of it. Finally, Thérèse ended the discussion by rather boldly stating, "My sister, if you look for the justice of God you will get it. The soul will receive from God exactly what she desires."[110]

Before the year was out, Sr. Fébronie caught the flu and died. Three months later, she appeared to St. Thérèse in a dream. Convinced that this was no ordinary dream, Thérèse reported it to the prioress, who documented it. Now follows that documented report in the saint's own words:

> O my Mother, my Sr. M. Fébronie came to me last night and asked that we should pray for her. She is in purgatory, *surely* because she had trusted too little in the mercy of the good Lord. Through her imploring behavior and her profound looks, it seemed she wanted to say, "You were right. I am now delivered up to the full justice of God but it is my fault. If I had listened to you I would not be here now."[111]

So, the moral of the story is that we can choose the path of justice or that of mercy. Yes, we really are free to choose — but also realize that the measure with which we measure will be measured back to us (see Lk 6:38). In other words, if we choose to treat others with strict justice, then God will be strict with us. If we choose to be merciful to others, then God will be merciful with us. *Hear that.* To choose the path of mercy means *being merciful to others.* This is one of the main efforts under the "keep trying" category for living the Little Way. So, let me repeat: To live the Little Way, we must be merciful to others. We must strive to show mercy. We must strive to forgive. Otherwise, we cannot hope for mercy (see Mt 5:7, 18:21-35).[112]

The second potential objection to making the Offering to Merciful Love has to do with those who have begun to feel that *they're in a bit too deep* with this Offering stuff. In other words, they may be saying,

> Look, I like the Divine Mercy message and devotion and everything, and I thought I'd do a nice little consecration. But I didn't know about "the catch" and all this talk about an "increased longing for God" and all that. Although this may not seem scary to others, it's making me nervous. I mean, *what am I getting myself into?*

In answer to that difficulty, let me say this: Yes, the Offering to Merciful Love is a powerful spiritual act, one that should be approached with a certain seriousness. However, keep in mind that the whole focus of the Offering is mercy and the God "who is all gentleness."[113] Having said that, I do have one suggestion if you're feeling a bit anxious about making it: Say the prayer, "Yes, Lord, I do want to be a saint, *but please be gentle*."[114] Frankly, that's a prayer I myself often pray, and I can assure you that the Lord has, indeed, been very gentle with me. But if that's not enough, then please consider Thérèse's own words about making the Offering to Merciful Love *as a little soul*:

> I am only a child, powerless and weak, and yet it is my weakness that gives me the boldness of offering myself as *VICTIM of Your Love, O Jesus!* In times past, victims, pure and spotless, were the only ones accepted by the Strong and Powerful God. To satisfy Divine Justice, perfect victims were necessary, but the *law of Love* has succeeded to the law of fear, and *Love* has chosen me as a holocaust, me, a weak and imperfect creature.[115]

Again, it's Thérèse's *weakness* that gave her the boldness to offer herself to Merciful Love. So, if you're feeling maybe too weak to make the Offering, that's a good thing. Also, recall that Thérèse's words here are similar to something else she said, which we read on Day 15: "What sweet joy it is to think that God is *Just*, i.e., that He takes into account our weakness, that He is perfectly aware of our fragile nature. What should I fear then?"[116] Good question. What should we fear? God is Love and Mercy itself, and the heart of the Little Way and the Offering is to *trust* in God. It's true that we're not going to fully understand the whole path. It's true that I cannot tell you exactly how it will all play out. But it will be wonderful. And if there's one thing that Thérèse wants to say to us, it's this: *trust*. Trust in God, who is Love and Mercy itself.

The third and final objection is one that may have arisen in response to the idea that the Offering to Merciful Love is a way of taking the rejected mercy that other people don't want.

Now, perhaps that seems selfish. Perhaps it makes us say, "But what about all those poor people who aren't getting the graces that I'm taking?" Well, first of all, keep in mind that the graces we'll be receiving *have already been rejected*. In other words, people have already said through their words or actions that they don't want them. So, these rejected graces are free for the taking.[117] Also, keep in mind that the Offering is far from selfish when we aim to do it, above all, to console Jesus. That was St. Thérèse's intention in making it, and it should be our intention as well. (More on this later.)

One more thing regarding the last objection: When we take the graces that others don't want, we're actually giving them a "second chance" to receive those graces. Why? Because, again, one of the effects of the Offering to Merciful Love is that it makes our hearts more compassionate. That means we'll be moved to pray for the conversion of hardened sinners — the very same ones who rejected the graces of mercy that we'll be receiving. And so, through our prayers and deeds of mercy that are the fruit of our Offering, they'll get a *second chance* to receive God's mercy.

Anyway, that covers three potential objections that may be coming to mind as we prepare to make the Offering. Tomorrow, we'll actually delve into Thérèse's masterpiece, the crowning of her Little Way: the text of her Offering to Merciful Love.

Today's Prayer:

Come, Holy Spirit, fire of mercy.
Take away any fears or anxieties I may have about making the Offering.

DAY 20
The Offering (Part One)

For the last two days of this week, we'll reflect on the actual text of St. Thérèse's Offering to Merciful Love, which consists of 11 paragraphs.[118]

The first paragraph, in which Thérèse describes the goal of her Offering, contains one of the best definitions of what it means to be a saint:

> (1) O My God! Most Blessed Trinity, I desire to *Love* You and make You *Loved*, to work for the glory of

> Holy Church by saving souls on earth and liberating those suffering in purgatory. I desire to accomplish Your will perfectly and to reach the degree of glory You have prepared for me in Your Kingdom. I desire, in a word, to be a saint, but I feel my helplessness and I beg You, O my God! to be Yourself my *Sanctity!*

Notice how, having stated the goal (becoming a saint), Thérèse clearly realizes that she is "helpless" when it comes to attaining it. So, in a bold move, she chooses to rely on *God's sanctity*, a choice that carries into the next paragraph:

> (2) Since You loved me so much as to give me Your only Son as my Savior and my Spouse, the infinite treasures of His merits are mine. I offer them to You with gladness, begging You to look upon me only in the Face of Jesus and in His heart burning with *Love.*

Here, we see that Thérèse does not want to rely on her own merits but, rather, on those of Jesus. And then, in the next paragraph, she also throws in the merits of the saints, angels, and the Blessed Mother.[119] (Why not?)

> (3) I offer You, too, all the merits of the saints (in heaven and on earth), their acts of *Love*, and those of the holy angels. Finally, I offer You, *O Blessed Trinity!* the *Love* and merits of the *Blessed Virgin, my dear Mother.* It is to her I abandon my offering, begging her to present it to You. Her Divine Son, my *Beloved* Spouse, told us in the days of His mortal life: "*Whatsoever you ask the Father in my name he will give it to you!*" I am certain, then, that You will grant my desires; I know, O my God! that *the more You want to give, the more You make us desire.* I feel in my heart immense desires and it is with confidence I ask You to come and take possession of my soul. Ah! I cannot receive Holy Communion as often as I desire, but, Lord, are You not *all-powerful?* Remain in me as in a tabernacle and never separate Yourself from Your little victim.

Thérèse's boldness in relying on the merits not only of God but of the saints and angels reaches new heights after she *reminds* the Lord of his promise in Scripture to grant whatever we ask. I say "new heights," because she actually asks God to "take possession" of her soul[120] and to sacramentally remain in her "as in a tabernacle." Can we even ask for that? Thérèse doesn't seem to have a problem with it.[121] After all, isn't God "all-powerful"? And isn't he the one who inspired these desires in the first place?

In the next paragraph, Thérèse states yet another desire and another bold petition:

> (4) I want to console You for the ingratitude of the wicked, and I beg of You to take away my freedom to displease You. If through weakness I sometimes fall, may Your *Divine Glance* cleanse my soul immediately, consuming all my imperfections like the fire that transforms everything into itself.

The bold *petition* is remarkable: Thérèse asks the Lord not only to take away her freedom to sin but to cleanse her from the stain of any falls as they happen. (Can we ask for that? Apparently so.) Thérèse's expressed *desire* is no less remarkable: She wants to "console" Jesus, a desire that she repeats later (see paragraph 6), a desire that's a particularly important concept in her spirituality.[122]

Actually, Thérèse's desire to console Jesus responds to an objection some might have, namely, that the goal of the Offering is selfishly all about Thérèse's own personal sanctity. Well, it's not. Again, it's about consoling Jesus. In other words, Thérèse wants to become a saint not to please herself but, rather, *to please Jesus.* Elsewhere in her writings, she makes this point clear:

> If the good God were to say to me: "If you die immediately, you will obtain great glory; if you die at the age of eighty, your glory will be far less, but it will please me much more," then I would not hesitate to answer: My God, I want to die at eighty for I am not seeking my own glory, but only to please You.[123]

Now, having made that clarification, I suggest we go back and reread just the first four paragraphs of the Offering itself, pondering them in our hearts for the remainder of today. Then, tomorrow, we'll reflect on the rest of the Offering.

Today's Prayer:

Come, Holy Spirit, fire of mercy.
Purify my intentions that I may do everything solely to please and glorify God.

DAY 21
The Offering (Part Two)

Yesterday, we covered the first four paragraphs of the text of the Offering to Merciful Love. Today, we'll read the remaining paragraphs, which begin with the topic of suffering:

> (5) I thank You, O my God! for all the graces You have granted me, especially the grace of making me pass through the crucible of suffering. It is with joy I shall contemplate You on the Last Day carrying the scepter of Your Cross. Since You deigned to give me a share in this very precious Cross, I hope in heaven to resemble You and to see shining in my glorified body the sacred stigmata of Your Passion.

Here, Thérèse speaks of suffering as a grace. That's because she understands that suffering can help unite us to our crucified Savior. But hers is not the unhealthy preoccupation with suffering that marked her early religious life. Rather, the focus in this paragraph is not on *seeking out* suffering but, rather, on *accepting* the suffering that *God* will choose for her. Accepting such suffering becomes easier when we learn from Thérèse just how loving and tender God really is. For instance, she tells us that God "cannot desire useless sufferings for us"[124] and that he even "shields his eyes" whenever we must endure it, because he doesn't want to have to see us suffer.[125]

> (6) After earth's Exile, I hope to go and enjoy You in the Fatherland, but I do not want to lay up merits for heaven. I want to work for *Your Love* alone with the one purpose of pleasing You, consoling Your Sacred Heart, and saving souls who will love You eternally.

As we learned earlier, Thérèse's way is not that of merit but of mercy and of love. In fact, we just read that her focus is on being merciful to Jesus and to her neighbor. In the next paragraph, it's clear why she doesn't worry about merits:

> (7) In the evening of this life, I shall appear before You with empty hands, for I do not ask You, Lord, to count my works. All our justice is stained in Your eyes. I wish, then, to be clothed in Your own *Justice* and to receive from Your *Love* the eternal possession of *Yourself*. I want no other *Throne*, no other *Crown* but *You*, my *Beloved!*

So, not wanting to gather merits with downward-facing, grasping hands, Thérèse wants to appear before the Lord with upward-facing, poor, and empty hands that are ready to receive God's gift of himself. And, again, she's not worried. Even if, along with her empty hands, she's full of weaknesses and imperfections, she does not fear. Why not? Well, because she knows *this* about God:

> (8) Time is nothing in Your eyes, and a single day is like a thousand years. You can, then, in one instant prepare me to appear before You.

Yes, he can do it. Simply recall what Thérèse had told her novice, Sr. Marie of the Trinity, who had asked if even she could hope to get to heaven right away after dying. Thérèse had responded, "Yes! God is so good. He will know how He can come and get you." He can "get" Sr. Marie, St. Thérèse, and all little souls by preparing us "in one instant" to appear before him.[126] And so, without any fear, Thérèse comes to the Offering itself:

> (9) In order to live in one single act of perfect Love, I OFFER MYSELF AS A VICTIM OF HOLOCAUST TO YOUR MERCIFUL LOVE, asking You to consume me incessantly, allowing the waves of *infinite tenderness* shut up within You to overflow into my soul, and that thus I may become a *martyr* of Your *Love*, O my God!

Ah, yes. In offering herself to Merciful Love and not justice, Thérèse opens herself to receive not waves of infinite harshness but "*infinite tenderness.*" Alright, but what does this have to do with living "in one single act of perfect Love?" We'll learn more about that in Appendix One. For now, however, on to martyrdom...

> (10) May this martyrdom, after having prepared me to appear before You, finally cause me to die and may my soul take its flight without any delay into the eternal embrace of *Your Merciful Love.*

Death and martyrdom? That sounds scary! Don't worry. To die of love is a beautiful thing. It's the way the Lord knows how he can come and "get" little souls at the end of their lives. Specifically, he'll lift the veil of his glory and approach us at the end with such a beautiful radiance of love and mercy that we won't be able to stand it. We'll long for him so ardently at that moment that our souls will, so to speak, "pop" out of our bodies and fly directly and immediately, without having to go through purgatory, into the embrace of his love.[127] That's the martyrdom of love, a martyrdom that, according to St. John of the Cross, is "very gentle and very sweet, sweeter and more gentle than [our] whole spiritual life on earth."[128] But until that blessed moment, Thérèse will continue to offer herself to Merciful Love:

> (11) I want, O my *Beloved*, at each beat of my heart to renew this offering to You an infinite number of times, until the shadows having disappeared I may be able to tell You of my *Love* in an *Eternal Face to Face!*[129]

Now, while I don't yet have a method for renewing the Offering to Merciful Love "at each beat of my heart," I can recommend an easy method for renewing it at each breath. (See Appendix One.)

Alright, so, let's spend today reflecting on the six paragraphs of the Offering that we covered today. Then, beginning tomorrow, we'll spend one full week in an Advent-like time of hope-filled darkness before reviewing everything we've learned and then actually making the Offering.

Today's Prayer:

Come, Holy Spirit, fire of mercy.

Fill my heart with a deeper and deeper longing for God, even unto the martyrdom of love.

Week Four

Into the Darkness

After making her Offering to Merciful Love, St. Thérèse was filled with consolation. She describes the feeling: "Ah! since the happy day, it seems to me that Love penetrates and surrounds me, that at each moment this Merciful Love renews me ... Oh! how sweet is the way of Love!"[130] *In fact, the year she made her offering truly was her "year of mercy."*[131] *We can call it that not only because she offered herself to Merciful Love and experienced its powerful effects but also because she spent the whole year writing the first installment of her autobiography (called Manuscript "A"). That work, which she began in obedience to her superior, Mother Agnes, helped her to see more clearly than ever God's tender mercies enveloping her whole life. In fact, it made her so filled with confidence in God's love for her that she concluded the manuscript as follows: "How will this 'story of a little white flower' come to an end? ... I don't know, but what I am certain about is that God's mercy will accompany her always."*[132]

We now know how Thérèse's story came to an end. From Good Friday 1896 until her death on September 30, 1897, she was immersed in darkness. Nevertheless, her trust in God's mercy during that time, and God's faithfulness to her, became the confirmation of her Little Way. This week, we'll explore the role that darkness plays in living it out.

DAY 22
The Darkness of Sin

One difficulty people often have with embracing the Little Way is that Thérèse wasn't much of a sinner. For instance, they say, "How can I relate to a nun who died at the age of 24 and whose confessor solemnly declared that she never committed a mortal sin?[133] Sure, she describes herself as full of weakness, imperfections, and faults, but those don't seem to include deliberate venial sins and certainly not mortal sins.[134] So, she doesn't really know the darkness of sin. I can't relate to her."

There's some truth to this objection. Although Thérèse certainly felt *capable* of committing grave sin, she believed that God's mercy had preserved her from it.[135] Also, one could easily conclude that her venial sins were not deliberate. For instance, let's hear some of the sins of she who sees herself as "weakness itself."[136] They included impatience with a sister, a missed opportunity to make a sacrifice, aversion to a medicinal drink, an interior movement of curiosity toward a magazine.[137] Surely these aren't the kinds of "sins" that thrust most people into discouragement!

The average Christian in our day struggles with attachments, addictions, deliberate venial sins, and even potentially grave sins. It's these kinds of sinners who often find themselves slipping into discouragement and even despair. It's these kinds of "ordinary" sinners who often have to fight the temptation to doubt God's tender love for them — and these are the fortunate ones! These are the ones who at least *recognize* their sins. But then there's the whole category of sinners who hardly see *any* sin in themselves. And because of this blindness to their own sins, such people, even more than others, hear about Thérèse and say, "I don't get her."

Now, regarding this latter, more serious kind of darkness, the "blindness to one's sins," we'll cover it tomorrow. For today, though, let's look at those who feel they can't relate to Thérèse or her teaching because they actually struggle with attachments, deliberate venial sins, and maybe even grave sins.

Thankfully, Thérèse anticipated their difficulty. She did so at the end of her autobiography with words we already read on Day 10, words that are worth repeating:

> Yes, I feel it; even though I had on my conscience all the sins that can be committed, I would go, my heart broken with sorrow, and throw myself into Jesus' arms, for I know how much He loves the prodigal child who returns to Him.[138]

"All the sins that can be committed." Think about that: That's *a lot* of sin. It includes my sins and your sins. But then, to make her point even clearer, Thérèse goes on, "It is not because God, in His anticipating Mercy, has preserved my soul from mortal sin that I go to Him with confidence and love."[139] And with that, her journal ends. The sickness that would take the young nun's life left her too weak to even write. But those last words are extremely telling. Thérèse is saying to us, "Yes! God kept me from committing mortal sin, but that's not why I feel such confidence in going to him. Even if I were the biggest sinner in the world, I would still go to him with a contrite heart and receive his mercy! *And so should you.*"

Thérèse so strongly wanted to make this point about God's great mercy that, even after she'd lost the strength to write, she basically pleaded with Mother Agnes to conclude the thought for her. In fact, several times, she urged her superior with words such as these:

> One could think that it is because I haven't sinned that I have such great confidence in God. Really tell them, Mother, that if I had committed all possible crimes, I would always have the same confidence. I feel that this whole multitude of offenses would be like a drop of water thrown into a fiery furnace. You will then tell the story about the converted sinner who died of love.[140]

In response to Thérèse's requests, here's what Mother Agnes later added to the manuscript, an addition that includes the "story about the converted sinner who died of love":

> No, there is no one who could frighten me,[141] for I know too well what to believe concerning His Mercy and His Love. I know that this whole multitude of sins would be lost in the twinkling of an eye like a drop of water cast into a burning furnace. In the lives of the desert fathers, it is told how one of them converted a public sinner whose evil deeds were the scandal of the whole country. Touched by grace, the sinful woman followed the Saint into the desert to perform a rigorous penance. On the first night of the journey, before even reaching the place of her retreat, the vehemence of her love and sorrow broke the ties binding her to earth, and at the same moment the holy man saw her soul carried by angels to

> God's bosom. This is a striking illustration of what I want to say, but the reality itself is beyond the power of words to express.[142]

We'll now let these last words of Thérèse's autobiography be the last words of this day's meditation. May they show us that in the light of God's Merciful Love, the darkness of sin (repented sin) is not so dark after all.

Today's Prayer:

Come, Holy Spirit, fire of mercy.
Let the light of God's Merciful Love
shine into the darkness of my sin.

DAY 23

The Blindness to Sin

Living the Little Way requires that we recognize our littleness. Problem is, many of us don't see it. As St. Thérèse put it, "We must be humbled and recognize our nothingness, *and that is what so many are not willing to do.*"[143] Now, that surely is true. There are certainly many people who are unwilling to "be humbled" and recognize their "nothingness." But today, I believe the bigger problem is that so many people *simply don't see it.* They sincerely don't realize that they're sinners. They're spiritually blind.

Let me put it this way: I'm a priest. I hear confessions. And let's just say there are a lot of people out there who are extremely spiritually blind. They'd almost have you believe that they were immaculately conceived, like Mary. For instance, after years of not going to Confession, people say things like, "Look, Father, I'm a good person. I don't have any sins."

Now, there are two problems here. First, they're wrong. They do have sins, and lots of them. The Bible says that even the just man sins seven times a day (Prov 24:16). Second, too many people think it's enough simply to be a "good person." Well, it's not enough! Jesus doesn't just want "good people" — he wants *saints.* He wants us to be *on fire* with his love, and anything less is not enough for him. For instance, the Lord's moving words from the Gospel of Luke come to mind: "I have come to set the earth on fire, and how I wish it were already blazing!" (12:49). Also, I can't help but think of his frightening words from the Book of Revelation: "So, because you are lukewarm, and neither hot nor cold, I will vomit you out of my mouth" (3:16).

Okay, so blindness to one's sin is a big problem today. And why is it a problem? Let me put it this way: the Good News isn't really news if we don't feel we're in need of it. I mean, why should we get excited about God's abundant mercy for sinners if we don't really think we're sinners? Why care about mercy if we don't feel we're in need of it? Why go to Confession when we've not done anything wrong? Well, we *have* done something wrong — and again, not just one thing, but lots of things. I mean, we're all sinners (see Rom 3:23, 1 Jn 1:8-10), and we all desperately need God's mercy.

Now, at this point, many of us may be enthusiastically agreeing, "That's right! We're all sinners!" In fact, we may even be congratulating ourselves: "Oh, thank goodness I'm not like those spiritually blind people. I clearly see my sins." But do we? Spiritual blindness extends even to those who recognize that they're sinners. Consider this: Jesus once told St. Faustina
Saint Faustina — "If I were to reveal to you the whole misery that you are, you would die of terror."[144] Now, I hesitate to bring up that quote, because I don't want little souls to begin beating themselves up and falling into discouragement. However, there's a deeply important truth here, and if we don't get it, we'll have a hard time living the Little Way.

Let me put it this way: Have you ever wondered why the great saints often spoke of themselves as being the biggest sinners? It doesn't seem to make any sense, right? So what do they see that we don't? For instance, apart from what we covered on Day 7, why does St. Thérèse, "the greatest saint of modern times," see herself as being such a *little* soul? Well, if we can discover the secret to her littleness, then we'll discover the secret to her sanctity. Okay, so here's the secret: *Thérèse realized that she could not compete with God*. Let me explain.

God wants us to love him as he loves us. In fact, Jesus even commands us to "be perfect as your heavenly Father is perfect" (Mt 5:48). And as I mentioned earlier, he wants us to be *on fire* with love. Now, St. Thérèse knew all this, so she tried to perfectly fulfill the commandment of love — but she couldn't do it. She realized that she couldn't compete with God's love. As she herself put it, compared to God's love for her, her love for him "is not even a drop of dew lost in the ocean!"[145] And the deeper she delved into the mystery of God's love for her, the more she realized she couldn't compete.[146] She clearly understood that she couldn't love God as he loved her. She knew that, compared to God, she'd always be a weak, pitiful lover.

So, the light that illumines the darkness of our spiritual blindness to our sins is the *fire* of God's love. Think of it: God loves us so much more than we love him. From the Cross, he cries out for love of us, "I thirst!" — and we mumble our prayers. He pours out his life for us in his Passion and Death — and we complain about a headache. His loving gaze is fixed on us night and day — and we hardly look at him. He does everything to please us — and we're focused on pleasing ourselves.

When we compare, then, the mystery of God's infinite, burning love for us with our own weak efforts to love him in return, it humbles us, lowers us, reduces us, and crushes us to the dust — but it doesn't destroy us.

Yes, I know it may seem that God's love would destroy us. After all, we just heard that Jesus told St. Faustina that she'd die of terror if he showed her all of her wretchedness. But here's some saving good news: *In his loving mercy, God fills up the abyss of our wretchedness with his own divine love.* This is St. Thérèse's amazing insight after she was conquered by love. As she herself expressed it to the Lord: "For me to love You as You love me, *I would have to borrow Your own love.*"[147]

And she knew he'd give it. She knew that after God conquers us and humbles us with his love, he then saves us with love by giving us his own divine love. In other words, after he flattens us with his overwhelming love, God then lifts us up and fills us with his love *so we actually can love him as he loves us*. In the end, then, we *can* compete. We *can* be perfect. We *can* be set *on fire*. (More on this tomorrow.)

Today's Prayer:

Come, Holy Spirit, fire of mercy.
Open the eyes of my heart with your love
that I may see my need for your Merciful Love.

DAY 24

Liturgical Darkness

Yesterday, we learned the secret to overcoming our blindness to our own personal sins, the secret to being little: *the fire of God's love*. We saw how that love humbles us, making us realize that we can't compete, that we can't love God as he loves us, that we can't be perfect as our heavenly Father is perfect.

Alright, so we're weak, little, pitiful lovers. We're sinners who would "die of terror" if we fully realized our selfishness and sin. Well, thank God, it doesn't end there.

Once we're humbled, God lifts us up. Again, as St. Thérèse said to the Lord, "For me to love you as you love me, *I would have to borrow your own love*." And she knew she could! Indeed, she was absolutely confident that God would allow her to borrow his own divine love. For evidence of this, we need only look as far as the text of her Offering to Merciful Love:

> I desire, in a word, to be a saint, but I feel my helplessness and I beg You, O my God! To be Yourself my *Sanctity!* … [L]ook upon me only in the Face of Jesus and in His heart burning with Love … [I]t is with confidence I ask you to come and take possession of my soul … Remain in me as in a tabernacle … All our justice is stained in Your eyes. I wish, then, to be clothed in Your own Justice and to receive from Your Love the eternal possession of Yourself … [Allow] the waves of infinite tenderness shut up within You to overflow into my soul.[148]

Clearly, Thérèse is confident that God will let her "borrow" his own love so she can love him perfectly in return. She knows that he himself will be her "*Sanctity*" and that God the Father will look upon her "only in the Face of Jesus and in His heart burning with *Love.*" She's confident that God's love will "take possession" of her and "remain" in her that she might be "clothed" in God's "own Justice" and filled with an "overflow" of the "infinite tenderness" of his love. She knows that "all our justice," that is, all our own efforts, are "stained" in God's eyes. So, her aim is to love God with his own perfect love.

But when will Thérèse get that love? When will she be able to love God perfectly with his own divine love? She believes it will be only at the moment of her death, when she hopes to be "*a martyr*" of God's Love. More specifically, she believes that her desires will be realized only in heaven: "What attracts me to the homeland of heaven is the Lord's call, the hope of loving Him finally as I have so much desired to love Him."[149] So, according to St. Thérèse, only in heaven will we love God with perfect love. Still, there's such a thing as *heaven on earth.* There's a time here on earth when we can love God perfectly with his own divine love: It's when we participate in the Holy Sacrifice of the Mass.

The Mass is, as it were, heaven on earth. It provides us the opportunity, in the veiled form of Sacrament, to love God as he loves us, to actually love him perfectly. Specifically, it happens during what I call the "supercharged" moment of the Mass. That's the moment when the priest at the altar takes the Body and Blood of Christ into his hands and offers it up to God the Father with these words: "Through him, and with him, and in him, O God, almighty Father, in the unity of the Holy Spirit, all glory and honor is yours forever and ever. Amen."

That moment is supercharged because, at the Mass, Jesus is giving himself Body and Blood, Soul and Divinity into our hands: *literally*, in the hands of the priest, and *spiritually*, in the hands of all the lay faithful who unite their own sacrifices to the offering of the priest at the altar. Then, together, each in his own way, we offer Jesus' infinite sacrifice of love to the Father and ourselves along with it.[150] That's the moment when Jesus' sacrifice becomes our sacrifice, when Jesus' love becomes our love, when Jesus' offering of himself becomes our offering of ourselves. So, in that moment, we love God perfectly with his own divine love. More specifically, we love the Father with the perfect love of the Son, in the unity of the Holy Spirit.

But, again, that experience of heaven on earth is hidden under the veil of a Sacrament. In other words, it takes place through the darkness of liturgical worship, a worship that points to and makes manifest the divine worship of heaven through the poverty of signs and symbols wrought by human hands. And while the Mass truly does make present the sublime worship of heaven, our eyes remain blind to the myriad of angels praising the Lord, the countless throng of saints gathered around the altar, and the overwhelming glory of Our Savior giving himself over to our loving and merciful Father. And yet, through the Mass, we truly and fully participate in that mystery. Through the Mass, we perfectly love God with "borrowed," infinite love — the divine love of the Son for the Father.

Today's Prayer:

Come, Holy Spirit, fire of mercy.

Help me to participate fully, consciously, and actively in the "borrowed" divine love of liturgical worship.

DAY 25
The Daily Darkness

Yesterday, we looked at our "daily bread" of the Mass, our way of entering heaven while still on earth, though in a veiled way. We saw how the Mass is our way of anticipating and participating in the perfect love of God for himself, and thereby, a way to become "perfect" ourselves. But there's another daily bread, a daily bread we also must share in if we are to live the Little Way: the bread of *daily darkness*.

Most of us are among the vast majority of humanity who are not famous, not well known, and not held up high on the pedestal of public opinion. In other words, we're probably numbered among "the ordinary people." If that describes you, then thank the Lord. It will be much easier for you to live the Little Way, become one of the greatest saints of all time, and help save the world. (More on that tomorrow.) But we have to be willing to accept the cross of an ordinary life and eat the bread of daily darkness. Let me explain.

Of course, most of us, especially in this social media age, long to be known, well liked, and praised for being important or attractive. But then, when we have to endure the torture of being quiet and alone in our own rooms,[151] we realize that in the eyes of the world, we're not so important or attractive. I mean, even if we have plenty of accomplishments and beautiful selfies, there will still be that self-accusing ache that creeps in and says, "You've not attained a destiny of greatness. You're not important. You're not attractive. You're *nothing*." To combat this, we may take even more selfies or rush off to accomplish even greater things to make a name for ourselves, to be "somebody." But the ache comes back because we can never do enough to satisfy our craving for greatness and love, and our precious "accomplishments" and digital images fade away like so much dust and vanity (Eccl 1:2).[152]

Now, make no mistake: We are called to be great, very great — beyond-our-wildest-imaginings great. But this greatness is not what's usually thought of as greatness. True greatness isn't based on the judgment and assessment of mortals. Rather, it's based on the judgment of Almighty God, who alone is truly great. And his greatness is revealed in the fact that what most attracts him are the little souls: the humble, the weak, and the broken. His greatness is shown in how he has "scattered the proud in their conceit and has lifted up the lowly" (Lk 1:51), in how he "resists the proud but gives grace to the humble" (Jas 4:6). And to little souls like us, if we accept it, his greatness is shown in the way that he will give us a share in his own greatness and glory.

But remember, the Little Way is a Little Way *of darkness*. So, we won't always feel the greatness of God filling our hearts. (If we did, we might get puffed up with pride and no longer be little.) In fact, most of the time, we probably won't feel it at all, and we'll have to fight to believe that God still loves us. In fact, we may have to fight depression, discouragement, and even despair. We may have to "hope against hope" in God's promise of mercy. And that's really the fine point of living the Little Way.

Little souls often live ordinary lives, but they're called to do so *with extraordinary faith, hope, and love.* Their extraordinary *faith and hope* is to believe in God's promise of mercy and to hope that he will bring them to the heights of holiness, even if neither they nor anyone else sees it in this life. Their extraordinary *love* consists in their efforts to keep trying, to keep striving to love God and neighbor in the little things. In fact, their aim is to do *little things with great love.*[153]

Now, in their efforts to live all this hidden and extraordinary faith, hope, and love, little souls are in good company. For instance, back on Day 4, we saw that Mary, the Mother of God, had to eat the daily bread of darkness. Think of that. This most blessed among women lived a hidden life in an unknown little town while bearing the same burdens of countless ordinary people. For instance, she cooked meals, changed diapers, and washed laundry. But in the midst of her hidden and ordinary life, she had an extraordinary faith, hope, and love.

Faith, hope, and love in the midst of the daily darkness: That was Mary's greatness, and that can be our greatness, too. So don't believe the voices of the world that say, "You're not important! You're not attractive! You're not successful! You're not anything!" With the Little Way, the Lord will make us immensely important, incredibly attractive, and wildly successful in his eyes — but we'll have to accept that we probably won't see it. We'll have to accept to be in the dark, to live an ordinary life, and to walk by faith. Yes, we'll simply need to embrace the promise that God will clothe us with his own divine love in his own time and in his own manner, even if we have to wait until the very end.

To close today's reflection, let's ponder Thérèse's description of the Little Way *as a way of darkness*:

> Jesus took me by the hand, and He made me enter a subterranean passage where it is neither cold nor hot,

> where the sun does not shine, and which the rain or the wind does not visit, a subterranean passage where I see nothing but a half-veiled light, the light which was diffused by the lowered eyes of my Fiancé's Face!
>
> My Fiancé says nothing to me ... I don't see that we are advancing toward the summit of the mountain since our journey is being made underground, but it seems to me that we are approaching it without knowing how.[154]

Today's Prayer:

Come, Holy Spirit, fire of mercy.
Help me to live my ordinary life
with an extraordinary faith, hope, and love.

DAY 26
The World's Darkness

This week, we've focused on better understanding the darkness of our own weakness, brokenness, and sin. And through that effort, we've come to find a light in the darkness, namely, *God's own love* that fills up the abyss of our nothingness.

Now, today, we're going to reflect on how the love that fills up the abyss of our nothingness also *overflows.* In fact, as we'll now learn, this overflowing love has the potential to engulf the entire world. I say it has "the potential," because *it's up to us* whether or not we'll let it. Alright, so here's a most important question: *Do you want to help save the world?*

Clearly, our world needs saving. As we learned on Day 13, in many ways we're living in a time of unprecedented darkness and evil. But for that very reason, in a sense, God is giving us unprecedented grace. In other words, *now is the time of mercy.* And guess what? During this blessed time, God wants to save the world by the power of Divine Mercy — *through us.* Let me explain.

As we also learned on Day 13, St. Thérèse is a prophet who teaches us that in the present time of mercy, God wants to work some of the greatest miracles of his mercy in the history of the world. How? By taking some of the littlest souls and making them into some of the greatest of saints. Okay, but why? Is it so we can walk around with little halos around our heads and have nice spiritual conversations? No. It's to save the world.[155] That's God's master plan in this time of mercy. He wants to save the world through a "legion" of little souls inspired by saints like Thérèse of Lisieux. And while St. Thérèse begged God for a "great number" of such souls, it actually doesn't take that many. It just takes you and me … and maybe one other person.

If that sounds like crazy talk, don't blame me — blame the devil! After all, it was the devil himself who said to St. John Vianney, "If there were three upon earth like you, my kingdom would be destroyed."[156] Just three! Or, don't blame the devil, blame Abraham, our father in faith. Remember how he spoke with God about Sodom and Gomorrah? He asked the Lord, "Suppose there are fifty righteous within the city; will you then destroy the place and not spare it for the fifty righteous who are in it?" (Gen 18:24). The Lord said he would spare it for their sake. But Abraham kept negotiating, "What about for the sake of 45?" "Yes, I'll spare it." 40? Yes. 30? Yes. 20? Yes. 10? Yes. Abraham stopped there, and because there weren't 10 righteous people in the city, it was destroyed. So, blame Abraham! After all, maybe he could have gotten the number down to just three.

Anyway, here's the point. Even though the world is immersed in darkness, our situation isn't hopeless. I mean, it doesn't take *that* many people to save the world. And why is that? Because, in a sense, *the world has already been saved.* In fact, Jesus Christ's suffering, death, and Resurrection was enough to save a gazillion worlds. However, as we learned on Day 7, the Lord relies on us to help bring his salvation to others, even to those at "the ends of the earth" (Acts 1:8).

Now, this doesn't mean we have to go on endless mission trips and pilgrimages. Rather, *we can be missionaries of Divine Mercy to the whole world through prayer.* That's why St. Thérèse, who never left the convent, was declared "Patron Saint of Missionaries and the Missions," along with St. Francis Xavier. And while Francis physically went to the ends of the earth through apostolic labors, Thérèse spiritually traveled the world *through prayer*. Specifically, her prayer of offering herself to Merciful Love caused God's mercy to overflow from her little soul and out to the whole world. So, imagine if at least three more of us lived the Offering to Merciful Love to the full!

But there's another extremely important prayer for the present time of mercy: the Chaplet of Divine Mercy. This prayer comes to us from St. Thérèse's friend, St. Faustina[157] — and it's *powerful*. In fact, you might say that, in a sense, it's the most powerful prayer there is. What? Isn't the Mass the most powerful prayer? Yes, and that's why the Chaplet is so mighty. The Chaplet is a kind of *extension* of the prayer of the Mass. More specifically, it's an extension of the most powerful moment of the Mass, what I earlier called the "supercharged" moment. It's that moment at Mass when, "through him, with him, and in him," the Body and Blood, Soul and Divinity of Jesus Christ is offered up to the Father as a perfect sacrifice of love. It's that moment at Mass when, in spiritual union with the priest at the altar, all the baptized can hold up Christ's perfect sacrifice of love to the Father *as their own sacrifice*.

Alright, so when we pray the Chaplet, the intention of this supercharged moment of the Mass becomes very focused. Specifically, it becomes *a plea for mercy*.[158] As we hold up Christ's perfect sacrifice of love to the Father, we cry out for mercy for ourselves *and for the whole world*. And the Father especially hears and answers such a perfect and moving prayer. (For more information on the Chaplet and how to pray it, see this endnote. [159])

So, that's the secret to saving the world. Inspired by Saints Thérèse and Faustina, it's to "borrow" the infinite merits of Christ on the Cross and to offer them as a perfect sacrifice of mercy for the whole world. And this easily can save the world. Why? Because while the sins of the world are finite, the mercy that flows from the sacrifice of Jesus on the Cross is *infinite*. For the sake of Christ's sorrowful passion, we just need at least *three* people calling out to the Father: "Have mercy on us and on the whole world!" That's the Chaplet. That's the way to save the world through the power of God's Merciful Love.[160]

You know, it really is true. Just a small army of little souls can effectively help God to save the world by receiving all the rejected mercy that other souls don't want (the Offering to Merciful Love) and by calling out for mercy as they "borrow" the infinite merits of Christ on the Cross (the Chaplet). So, once again, *do you want to help save the world?*

Today's Prayer:

Come, Holy Spirit, fire of mercy.
Inspire me to help save the world
as a prayerful missionary of Divine Mercy.

DAY 27
Thérèse's Darkness (Part One)

Yesterday, we focused on the world's darkness and the ways that we can help save the world through Divine Mercy. But perhaps we moved on too quickly from the world's darkness to the light of mercy. Perhaps we didn't stop long enough to get a good grasp on what the world's darkness is all about. Well, that's what we're going to do today. More specifically, we're going to reflect on the root of the world's darkness and how it affected St. Thérèse.

Of course, the root of the world's darkness is sin. But why is there sin? Going back to the beginning, back to Day 1, we learned that sin comes from a lack of trust in God's goodness, a lack of faith in God and his Word. So, that's the deep root of the world's darkness. It's where people live as if God did not exist, as if there's no heaven, as if this world is all there is.

Well, such an empty, faithless, cynical worldview dominated St. Thérèse's 19th-century France and helped make atheism and godlessness more popular than ever before. Yet despite the fact that Thérèse lived behind the protective walls of a convent, God decided not to shield her from the dark and terrible sadness of the modern world.

Still, in his loving mercy, the Lord waited until she was ready. He waited until after she had discovered her Little Way and had offered herself to Merciful Love. In other words, he waited until her foundation on Divine Mercy was rock solid. Thérèse herself explains God's goodness in waiting:

> Never have I felt before this ... how sweet and merciful the Lord really is, for He did not send me this trial until the moment I was capable of bearing it. A little earlier I believe it would have plunged me into a state of discouragement.[161]

Okay, but what, specifically, was this trial that the Lord sent to Thérèse? The saint herself describes it as follows:

> I was enjoying such a living faith, such a clear *faith*, that the thought of heaven made up all my happiness, and I was unable to believe there were really impious people who had no faith. I believed they were actually speaking against their own inner convictions when they denied the existence of heaven, that beautiful heaven where God Himself wanted to be their Eternal Reward. During those very joyful days of the Easter season, Jesus made me feel that there were really souls who have no faith, and who, through the abuse of grace, lost this precious treasure, the source of the only real and pure joys. He permitted my soul to be invaded by the thickest darkness, and that the thought of heaven, up until then so sweet to me, be no longer anything but the cause of struggle and torment.[162]

Clearly, Thérèse was dealing with a night *of faith*, a trial *of faith*. But the other key word of this trial is "*heaven*," which is very interesting. After all, that cuts right to the heart of the Little Way, which is really all about heaven. I mean, as a "way," it goes *somewhere*. But where? To heaven. Indeed, the goal of Thérèse's way is heaven. Now, as we've learned, the threefold means to that goal involve trusting, trying, and *recognizing*. Recognizing what? Recognizing the darkness that comes from being little, helpless, and weak.

So, up to the time of her trial of faith, which she describes above, the darkness of Thérèse's Little Way was really about recognizing her helplessness and feeling incapable of the works of holiness. But that darkness eventually became Thérèse's joy, because she firmly believed and *trusted* that God would come down and raise her to the heights of heaven. After all, that's what mercy does. It goes to the lowest place and raises up.

But with Thérèse's trial of faith, the challenge of *trusting* became not just about her own darkness (the darkness of her littleness) but about a *deeper* darkness that attacked the very goal of her faith, hope, and love. I mean, it was no longer just about trusting in God's promise that he would raise her to the heights. Rather, it had to do with simply trusting that there *is* a heights, that there *is* a God, that there *is* a heaven. It was about trusting amid the darkness of not seeing the goal, not desiring the goal, and not feeling the slightest bit of joy at the thought of the goal.

Because Thérèse still trusted God, even in the face of this trial of double darkness — the darkness of her own helplessness and the darkness of temptations against God and heaven — she truly deserves the blessing given to Abraham and Mary. Indeed, she's blessed because she believed in God's promise of mercy that he would raise her to the heights of holiness, even though she was helpless and even though it seemed to her that there was no God and no heaven. She truly "hoped against hope," and she kept on hoping, trusting, and believing until the very end, as we'll see tomorrow.

Today's Prayer:

Come, Holy Spirit, fire of mercy.
Help me to trust even amid
the double darkness of my weakness
and temptations against God and heaven.

DAY 28
Thérèse's Darkness (Part Two)

Before yesterday, we may have thought that we couldn't relate to St. Thérèse because she lived in a convent and had no difficulties believing in God and heaven. We may have thought, "Well, she didn't live where I live. I mean, here it seems as if *nobody* believes in God, and living by faith is hard." But now we know that Thérèse also suffered the temptation to wonder whether there even is a God and a heaven. On top of that, she also felt rejected by God because of her sinfulness. And so, she bore both of those temptations, and not just for a day but for more than a year. Yet she "hoped against hope," trusting that God does exist and that he would make her into a great saint. But how did she do it? How do *we* do it? How do we persevere in faith, hope, and love in the midst of deep spiritual darkness? It's simple. Let me explain with an image that Thérèse herself used.

All of us, at one time or another, have basked in the rays of God's love (called by St. Ignatius of Loyola "consolation"). For instance, maybe we felt it at Mass when we received Holy Communion, when we read a passage from God's Word, when we stood before a majestic sunset, or when we received the tender love of a spouse, parent, or friend. Whenever it was, we've all experienced God's love and how real that love is. We've "seen" the divine sun and have been warmed by its rays.

But the problem is *we forget*. Dark clouds creep in and cover up the sun (what St. Ignatius calls "desolation"). We stop feeling its rays. We wonder if the sun is still up there. And perhaps we begin to get discouraged as our faith and trust start to waver and change to doubt and distrust.

Now, the difference between many of us and St. Thérèse is that she *clung* to God's promises of mercy and the memory of his love (consolation), especially in the midst of darkness (desolation).[163] She didn't give up. She kept trying. She kept trusting throughout the darkness. In short, she discovered her Little Way, and then her faith was tested, and then she passed the test — every day, to the very end.

So, truly blessed is she who believed that what was spoken to her by the Lord would be fulfilled! Truly blessed is she who clung to the memory of God's love in the midst of darkness! Truly blessed is she who provides us with such a personal and perfect example of trust!

And we *know* she was blessed. How do we know that? Well, read the following account of her death from Mother Agnes, and realize that St. Thérèse didn't die of tuberculosis. No, she *suffered* from tuberculosis, but she died of *love*.

> Her breathing suddenly became weaker and more laboured. She fell back on the pillow, her head turned towards the right … [S]he pronounced very distinctly her final act of love: "Oh! I love him … " she said, looking at her crucifix. Then a moment later: "My God … I … love you!"
>
> We thought that was the end, when, suddenly, she raised her eyes, eyes that were full of life and shining with an indescribable happiness "surpassing all her hopes." [That] sublime gaze … lasted for the space of a "Credo."
>
> … Then she closed her eyes and the whiteness of her face, which had become more accentuated during the ecstasy, returned to normal. She appeared ravishingly beautiful and had a heavenly smile.[164]

Remember that smile. Let it be a sign for you. As Abraham had the stars and Mary had the words of Elizabeth, you have Thérèse's smile. So, in times of darkness, when you're tempted to discouragement because of your own weakness, brokenness, and sin — remember that smile. In times of darkness, when you're tempted to think that God and heaven do not exist — remember that smile. In times of darkness, when you're tempted to think there's no way you can become a saint — remember that smile.

And, actually, Thérèse is smiling at you now. With her prayers, she's preparing your heart to accept the gift of the Offering to Merciful Love. She's telling you not to be afraid. She's saying, "I do not regret having offered myself to Love — and neither will you!"[165] And she's asking you to let her do good for you and to fulfill her mission in you, a mission that she expressed shortly before her death:

> I feel especially that my mission is about to begin, my mission to make God loved as I love him, to give my little way to souls. If God grants my desires, my heaven will be spent on earth until the end of time. Yes, I want to spend my heaven doing good on earth.[166]

We know that God granted the desires of this "greatest saint of modern times." So, will you let her help you? Will you let her give you the gift of the Little Way and her Offering to Merciful Love?

Today's prayer:

Come, Holy Spirit, fire of mercy.

Witness that I choose to accept St. Thérèse's help
as I prepare to offer myself to Merciful Love.

1877.

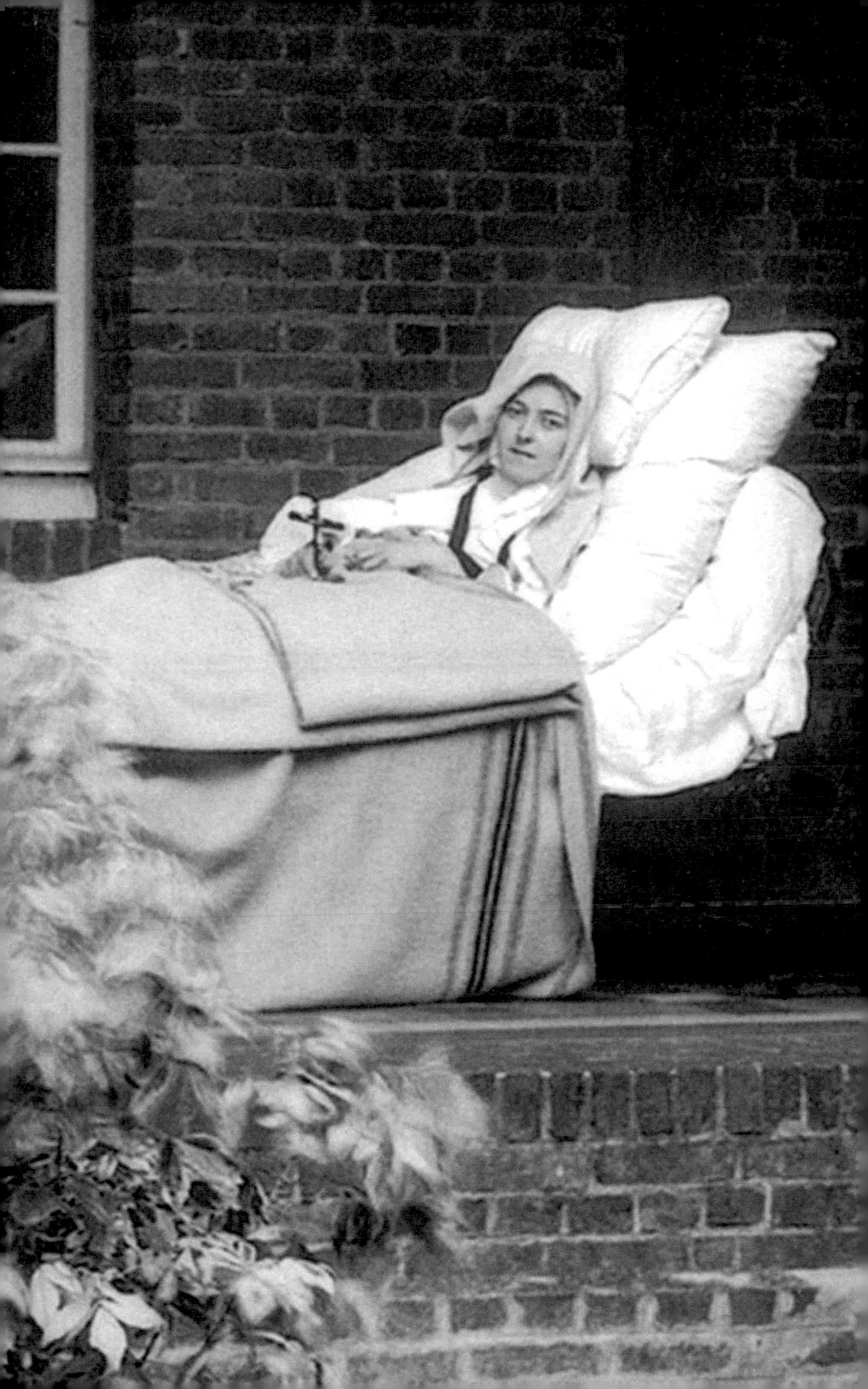

AU SOI
DE CETTE VIE
SEREZ JUGÉS
L'AMOUR
S. J. DE

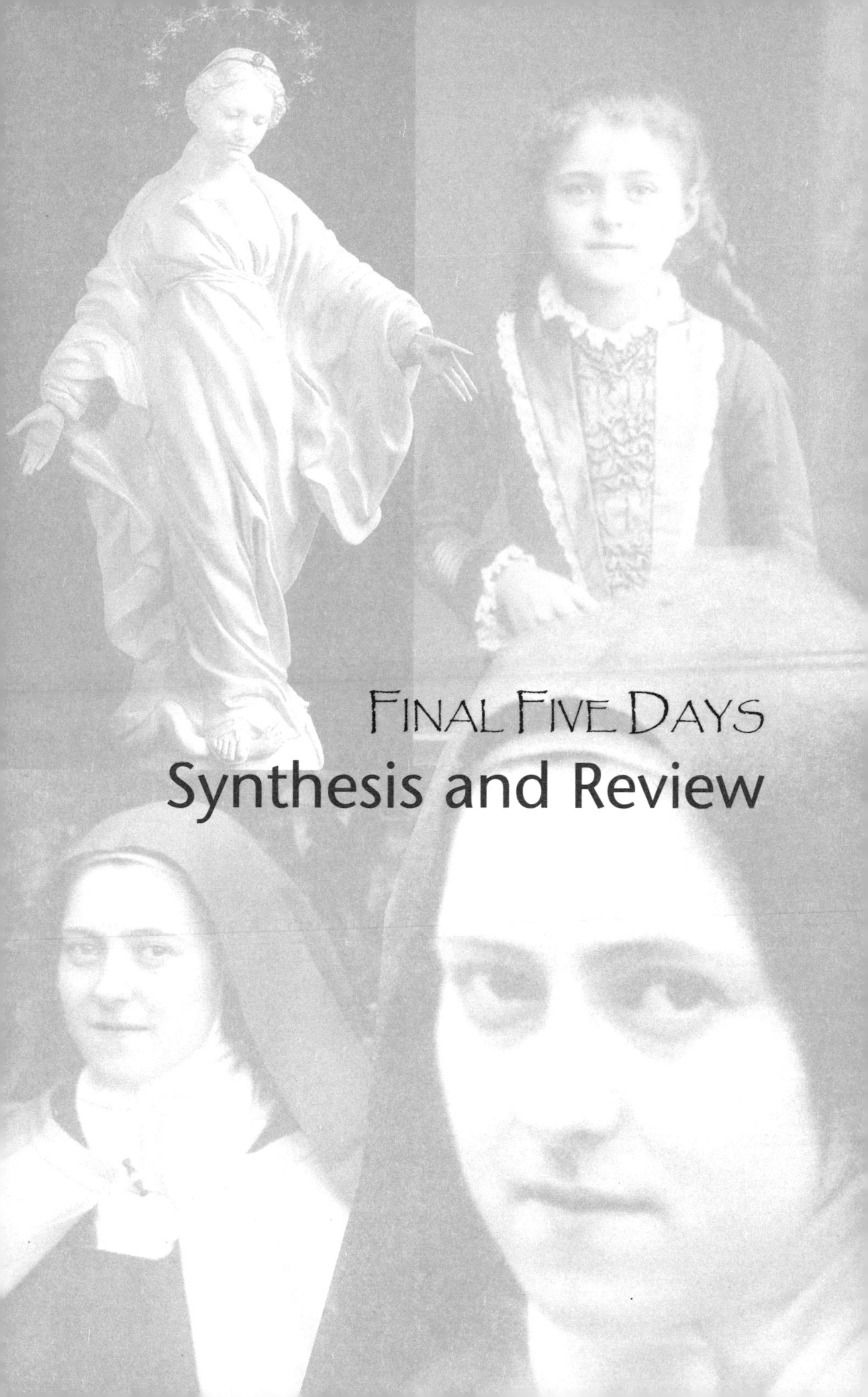

Final Five Days
Synthesis and Review

For four weeks, we've been reflecting on what a consecration to Divine Mercy (St. Thérèse-style) is all about — and we've covered a lot of material. While our prayer program of daily pondering the text has helped us digest some of the information, we can still go deeper. To do this, we need what St. John Paul II calls Mary's "wise capacity for remembering and embracing in a single gaze of faith."[167] *We can develop this "wise capacity" by continuing what we've been doing all along, namely, pondering in our hearts (see Lk 2:19), but now with a more refined focus.*

To give us this more refined focus, for each week of the retreat, I've chosen three words that summarize a given week's teaching. So, over the next four days, we'll reflect on three words each day, pondering their meaning for our Divine Mercy consecration. I'm confident that if we dedicate ourselves to this more refined prayer pondering, we'll be able to embrace the truth of this consecration "in a single gaze of faith." Then, after these four days of review, we'll read a synthesis of what we've learned in a single formula of consecration that aims to capture the essence of Thérèse's Offering to Merciful Love.

DAY 29

What Is Trust?

Three words summarize what we learned about trust: (1) Distrust, (2) Blessing, and (3) Grace.

DISTRUST

Of course, distrust is the opposite of trust. So, what can it tell us about trust? Actually, a lot. I say that because the word "distrust" reminds us that *we have a trust problem.* It reminds us that trust does not come naturally to us. It reminds us of what went wrong and helps us recognize the path to making things right.

Recall that our trust problem began with the fall of Adam and Eve. More specifically, it began with a lie: Eve listened to the lie of the serpent, a lie that made God seem jealous, selfish, and conniving. In other words, it called into question *God's goodness.* Thus, Adam and Eve, and we ourselves, are "afraid of the God of whom [we] have conceived a distorted image … ."[168]

The key to overcoming our trust problem has to do with "undistorting" our image of God. It's to begin to recognize the truth of God's goodness. And when we clearly see that God is good, merciful, and trustworthy, we begin to trust him. Of course, as we've already learned, St. Thérèse helps us with this. She provides powerful testimony to how good and truly merciful God is.

Blessing

Recall that, according to St. John Paul II, "*a kind of 'key'* unlocks for us the innermost reality of Mary." That key is the blessing of Elizabeth at the Annunciation: "Blessed is she who believed that what was spoken to her by the Lord would be fulfilled" (Lk 1:45). That blessing reveals the "innermost reality of Mary," because Mary's inner reality was a reality of *faith* (or *trust*). And the essence of faith is to believe God's Word.

More specifically, it's to believe that God is faithful to his promises, to believe that God is faithful even when it seems impossible. For instance, it's to "hope against hope," like Abraham did when he was called to sacrifice Isaac, believing in the impossible, namely, that God could even raise Isaac from the dead. It's to "hope against hope," like Mary did at the Cross, believing in the impossible, namely, that God could even raise Jesus from the dead. It's to "hope against hope" in our daily lives, when all is darkness and we're tempted to disbelieve in God's loving presence in our lives, tempted to doubt that "all things work together for good to those who love God" (Rom 8:28). It's to praise and thank God in all circumstances, because while we may not always understand his ways, "we know and believe the love God has for us" (1 Jn 4:16). And for such belief, for such hoping against hope in darkness, for such praising and thanking God in all circumstances, we, too, like Abraham and Mary, will be richly blessed.

GRACE

Mary is not only a perfect model of faith and trust for us, *but she obtains for us the grace to believe and to trust in God.* She does this through her powerful prayers for us, which are so effective because of the suffering she endured at the foot of the Cross.

There, Mary's Immaculate Heart was pierced with a sword as she beheld the agony of her Son. And from her pierced Heart, we obtain the grace to have hearts that open up to receive the love and mercy pouring forth from the Sacred Heart of Jesus (see Lk 2:35). Of course, Mary's Heart is not the source of grace and mercy, but the love of her Heart helps move us to open our hearts to receive God's gifts. Thus, Mary is the New Eve who brings us to the New Adam on the new tree of life, the Cross, and encourages us not to eat forbidden fruit of disobedience and distrust but to drink from the blessed fountain of eternal life, the Fountain of Grace and Mercy.

We need Mary's help to obtain the gift of faith, that is, the grace to believe. Also, in a certain sense, even God needs her help. I say that because our "trust problem" primarily has to do with God. But Mary isn't God — she's our tender, loving mother. And who could be afraid of such a mother? Thus, Mary is a kind of "secret weapon" for God, a way for his grace to enter hardened hearts, hearts that she then opens up to God.

Today's Prayer:

> *Spend the day pondering the meaning of trust as it is summarized in these three words: Distrust, Blessing, and Grace.*

DAY 30

The Little Way

Three words summarize what we learned about the Little Way. Put differently, we just need to remember to do three things: (1) Recognize, (2) Trust, and (3) Try.

Recognize

To live the Little Way, *we need to recognize the darkness of our littleness and our brokenness.* Remember, the Little Way is based on St. Thérèse's deep rediscovery of the heart of the Gospel, namely, God's mercy for sinners, God's love that goes out especially to the weak, broken, and sinful. Thérèse simply realized that by recognizing her littleness and helplessness more and more, she would, thereby, be more and more ready for the cascading love pouring forth from the pierced Heart of Jesus. In her Letter 197, she powerfully expresses this idea:

> [T]he weaker one is, without desires or virtues, the more suited one is for the workings of this consuming and transforming Love ... [B]ut we must consent to remain always poor and without strength, and this is the difficulty ... Ah! let us remain then *very far* from all that sparkles, let us love our littleness, let us love to feel nothing, then we shall be poor in spirit, and Jesus will come to look for us [and] He will transform us in flames of love.

Trust

Recognizing our weakness, brokenness, and sin can be a difficult thing. In the above quote, Thérèse even says, "This is the difficulty." And why is it difficult? It's difficult because the wound in each one of us, caused by original sin, makes us tend to doubt God's goodness and love. Indeed, we tend to think in a worldly, Jansenist way that says we must earn God's love by being perfect, strong, and without sin.

So, "the difficulty" is to reverse this tendency in ourselves and *to trust.* It's to ignore the "thieves of hope" and to believe in God's promise of mercy. It's to hope against hope that the Lord's Merciful Love goes out to us not because we're perfect, strong, and without sin, but because we're imperfect, weak, and sinful. In fact, it's to trust *even beyond that.* It's to trust the prophetic word of St. Thérèse of Lisieux, Doctor of the Church, that *God will satisfy our desires for holiness and raise us to the heights of sanctity.* It's to trust that he will make us into great saints, even if we don't see it happening, even if we struggle with the same sins day after day, even if we have to wait for the grace of great holiness until the very end of our lives. It's to believe Thérèse's word in Letter 197 that "it is confidence and nothing but confidence that must lead us to Love." It's to trust the word of the greatest saint of modern times when she tells us in that same letter that her "only treasure" is "the blind hope that I have in [God's] mercy." It's to listen to her ask us, "Why can't that treasure be ours?" And it's to realize, "That treasure can be mine, if I cling to God's mercy with trust."

TRY

So, to live the Little Way, we must recognize our weakness and trust in God's mercy — and we must also *keep trying.*

Okay, but what does that mean? It means we have to keep striving to grow in holiness. For instance, it means going to Mass and Confession regularly, taking time to pray, and doing little things with great love. It means forgiving those who have hurt us. It means being sorry for our sins, making a firm resolution not to sin again, and never making a "truce" with sin. It means not settling for complacency or mediocrity or the attitude that says, "Well, that's just who I am." In other words, it means striving to be faithful to examining our consciences every day. Also, it means not giving in to discouragement or, God forbid, despair. It means that if we fall into discouragement or despair, we'll make an effort to get right back up, right back to trusting in God's mercy. It means trying to remember and keep before our eyes the infinite mercy of God who never tires of forgiving. It means striving to never tire of asking God for forgiveness.

Today's Prayer:

> *Spend the day pondering how to live the Little Way as it is summarized in these three words: Recognize, Trust, and Try.*

DAY 31
The Offering

Three words summarize what we learned about the Offering to Merciful Love: (1) Console, (2) The Catch, and (3) Purgatory.

Console

The essence of the Offering to Merciful Love is to console the Heart of Jesus by accepting all the Merciful Love that other souls don't want. It's to see that Jesus' Heart aches because he wants to pour out his Merciful Love to sinners, but so many just don't want to receive it. It's to let him pour out that rejected love into our own sinful but contrite hearts.

In sum, through the Offering, we console Jesus by letting him love us. And this consoling love can make us into saints, even great saints. After all, what is holiness but the Merciful Love of God poured into our hearts? (See Rom 5:5.)

And while Thérèse begins her Offering to Merciful Love by expressing her desire to become a saint, she wants to become one specifically *to console the Heart of Jesus*, who longs to make us holy through his Merciful Love. Yes, Jesus wants us to receive the grace that makes us holy, and when we do, it consoles him, as he told St. Faustina:

> I desire to bestow My graces upon souls, but they do not want to accept them. You, at least, come to Me as often as possible and take these graces they do not want to accept. In this way you will console My Heart.[169]

The Catch

Alright, but if we offer ourselves to Merciful Love, what's the catch? I mean, if we receive all the rejected mercy that other souls don't want, what's that going to cost us? What's going to happen to us? Of course, there's a big catch when it comes to the offering to Divine Justice: lots of suffering! So what's the catch when we offer ourselves to Merciful Love? Well, there is, indeed, a catch, but it's not a scary one. The catch is that we accept to allow God's Merciful Love to gradually heal our hardened hearts, so they'll become more sensitive, compassionate, and loving. The catch is that our hearts will begin to become more as they should be: deeply moved by the suffering of others. And that's a beautiful thing! It's a beautiful thing to be moved by the suffering of the Heart of Jesus. It's a beautiful thing to be moved by the suffering of our neighbor. It's a beautiful thing to "weep with those who weep" (Rom 12:15) and to "comfort those who are in any affliction" with the same consolation we have received in Christ (see 2 Cor 1:4).

Now, while it's beautiful to have a compassionate heart, it does hurt. After all, the very definition of compassion is "to suffer with." But this kind of suffering is not so scary. Why not? Because such suffering, by its very nature, is other-directed. And when our focus is not on ourselves when we're suffering, while it certainly still hurts, we often don't even notice our own pain. We're too focused on the beloved who suffers.

In sum, then, here's the catch: It's to accept to have a heart that's more loving, compassionate, and merciful. And while having such a heart does cause us more pain, it's a bittersweet pain, the pain of compassion. Also, keep in mind that the alternative is terrible: a cold, hard, and distant heart that resists suffering with others, that resists being part of the Christian life of love.

Purgatory

Here's one other catch that comes with making the Offering to Merciful Love: It gradually increases our longing for God. Now, according to St. Faustina, such longing is the great suffering of purgatory.[170] But here, in this life, such longing is not as bad. In fact, it's a beautiful longing of love, a longing that purifies us at every moment and deepens our life of prayer. It's a longing that prepares us for the "martyrdom of love."

The martyrdom of love is the sweet martyrdom through which little souls can hope that God will come for us at the very end of our lives and manifest his love for us in such a way that it will cause us to die of love. In other words, seeing the overwhelming beauty of God's love, our souls will be so attracted to him that they won't be able to resist "jumping" into the embrace of his Merciful Love. Moreover, such a martyrdom is "very sweet"[171] and purifies the soul completely, leaving no trace of sin or punishment, which means it will not have to pass through the fire of purgatory.

According to St. Thérèse, such a remarkable gift of sanctity is relatively easy to obtain, even for very imperfect souls. Simply recall the case of Sr. Marie of the Trinity, one of St. Thérèse's novices who feared purgatory and wondered if someone as weak as she could hope to avoid it. After she asked if it were possible even for someone like her to hope to go straight to heaven after death, Thérèse replied, "Yes! God is so good. He will know how He can come and get you. But despite this, try to be faithful, so that He does not have to wait in vain for your love."[172]

Today's Prayer:

Spend the day pondering the Offering to Merciful Love as it is summarized in these three words: Console, the Catch, and Purgatory.

DAY 32
The Darkness

Three words summarize our week of going "into the darkness": (1) Relate, (2) See, and (3) Smile.

Relate

Saint Thérèse doesn't always make a good first impression. In fact, I've often heard that when people first meet her in her writings, they think, "I can't relate to her." They say, "What do I have in common with a girl who grew up in a sheltered home, lived in a cloistered convent, and died at just 24-years-old?" But then, as they get to know her more, they'll often say, "I relate to her more than to any other saint."

So, why do people relate so much to someone who, on the surface, seems difficult to relate to? I think it's because, even though she apparently never committed a mortal sin, she was absolutely convinced that, had God not sheltered her from an early age, she would have been a big sinner. And we believe her. We believe her particularly when she tells us that even if she had been a bigger sinner than we are, even if she had committed *all the sins that could be committed*, "I would go, my heart broken with sorrow, and throw myself into Jesus' arms, for I know how much he loves the prodigal child who returns to him."[173] Somehow, we relate to all that, or at least we want to. We relate to Thérèse because she's real, because she's not a plaster statue high on a pedestal. In fact, we get the sense that she's right down here in the grittiness of ordinary life with the rest of us.

Speaking of ordinary life, we can also relate to Thérèse's ordinariness. During her life, she wasn't famous or well known. Indeed, her time in the convent truly was a "hidden life" full of the daily darkness we all experience. Yes, she's a great saint, but her standout sanctity is that she did little things with great love. Yes, in the midst of an ordinary, mundane life, she had extraordinary faith, hope, and love that are accessible to us all. As she herself put it, "Why would this treasure not be yours?"[174]

Finally, we relate to Thérèse's double darkness. In other words, like most of us, she not only knew herself to be weak and imperfect (more on that in the next point), but she knew what it was like to live in an age of secularism and doubt. And she knew it not because she actually lived in that world — as a cloistered nun, she did not — but, rather, because the Lord allowed her to feel that God doesn't exist and that there isn't a heaven. That was her night of faith. Still, in the midst of such darkness, she clung to the Lord with faith, hope, and love and encourages us to do the same.

SEE

Thérèse solves the mystery as to why the great saints see themselves as great sinners. She also solves the mystery as to why so many sinners are often so blind to the fact that they're sinners.

It has to do with the reality of God's love — his burning, passionate, infinite love. Because great saints clearly see this reality, they're not blind to their sins. Because people who don't think they're sinners don't clearly see the reality of God's love, they're blind to their sins. But if they did see the reality of his love, their eyes would be opened to their sinfulness.

To put it differently, Thérèse teaches us that when we clearly see the reality of God's passionate love for us, it makes us realize we can't compete! It reveals that when we compare God's infinite love for us with our own pitiful love for him, our love is really *nothing*. But Thérèse doesn't leave us hanging. She tells us that God's love for us is so great that he allows us to "borrow" his own love.

Now, according to Thérèse, we don't fully borrow the Lord's perfect love until we get to heaven — by heaven, I mean both "heaven-heaven" (where we go when we die) and "heaven-on-earth" (where we go on Sundays). Of course, regarding that latter heaven, I'm talking about the Mass, which is where we can love God the Father through, with, and in the Son's own perfect love (and even "see" that love in Sacrament).

Smile

Remember Thérèse's smile at her death. Let it be a sign for you. As Abraham had the stars and Mary had the words of Elizabeth, you have Thérèse's smile. So, in times of darkness, when you're tempted to discouragement because of your own weakness, poverty, and sin — remember that smile. In times of darkness, when you're tempted to think that God and heaven do not exist — remember that smile. In times of darkness, when you're tempted to think there's no way you can become a saint — remember that smile.

And, actually, Thérèse is smiling at you now. With her prayers, she's preparing your heart to accept the gift of the Offering to Merciful Love. She's telling you not to be afraid. She's saying, "I do not regret having offered myself to Love — and neither will you!" So get ready. The day of your offering is just around the corner! All that rejected mercy will soon be yours. So don't forget to smile.

Today's Prayer:

Spend the day pondering the Offering to Merciful Love as it is summarized in these three words: Relate, See, and Smile.

DAY 33

Putting It All Together

For the last four days, we've been reviewing the last four weeks of our retreat. During those days, we've not only been reviewing the material, but we've also begun to put together all that we've learned. I say we've "begun" to put it all together. By that, I mean we're probably not yet at a point where we can grasp the Little Way and the Offering to Merciful Love "in a single gaze," as St. John Paul II put it. To get to that point, a unifying statement to summarize the main points of what we've learned may be helpful.

Actually, I think we need more than just a statement. We need a prayer — something we can frequently repeat, even every day, something that not only reminds us of the meaning of the Offering to Merciful Love but that also allows us to make it.

Now, of course, as we learned on Days 20 and 21, St. Thérèse has already composed such a marvelous prayer. And that may be the text you'd like to use and pray with, even daily. (See pages 135-137 for the full text.) However, while I do recommend privately praying Thérèse's actual prayer at least once (preferably on your consecration day), I dare say that there are two difficulties with using it under other circumstances: (1) It's rather long, and so it may not be practical for everyone to use as a daily prayer. (2) It doesn't clearly highlight all of the teachings we've covered during this retreat. Alright, well, because we're looking for a unifying statement, something that can summarize the main points of what we've learned, it may be helpful to have something more.

Okay, so here we seem to have a case where "less" is "more." In other words, it may be better to have something that's shorter (less) than Thérèse's text of Offering and that will also summarize all the main teachings we've covered during this retreat (more). Alright then, without any further ado, here's such a prayer — the Prayer of Consecration to Merciful Love:

> Merciful Father, relying on the prayers and example of Abraham and Mary, my father and mother in faith, and of St. Thérèse, my sister in the way of humble confidence, I, ____________________, choose, this day, with the help of your grace, to strive with all my heart to follow the Little Way. And so,
>
> > I firmly intend to fight discouragement, do little things with great love, and be merciful to my neighbor in deed, word, and prayer.
> >
> > I aim to keep before my eyes my poverty, weakness, brokenness, and sin, trusting that my littleness and contrite heart will attract your Merciful Love.
> >
> > I choose to remain always little, not relying on my own merits but solely on yours, dear Lord, and those of the Blessed Mother.[175]
> >
> > Finally, I believe, my God, that you can and will make me into a saint, even if I won't see it, even if I have to struggle all my life against vice and sin, even if I have to wait until the very end. This blind hope in your mercy, O Lord, is my only treasure.
>
> And now, to confirm my resolve and to console you for so much rejection of your mercy, I OFFER MYSELF, THROUGH THE HANDS OF MARY IMMACULATE,[176] AS A VICTIM OF HOLOCAUST TO YOUR MERCIFUL LOVE, asking you to consume me incessantly, allowing the waves of *infinite tenderness* shut up within you to overflow into my soul, and that I may thus become a *martyr*

> of your *love*, O my God, and a gift of mercy to so many others.
>
> I ask all this in Jesus' name. Amen.

So, there you have it: A compact prayer that expresses both the essence of Thérèse's Offering and the other main ideas of this retreat. For instance, do you see the essence of the Offering reflected in the last main paragraph? And can you make out the other main ideas in the middle paragraphs?

Great. But maybe you're looking for something even more compact. I mean, we've got the very long option (Thérèse's actual text), but what about a very short option? What about something that we can easily memorize and pray anytime during a busy day? Thankfully, Thérèse herself gives us such an option through a prayer she asked a dearly beloved friend to pray for her during the last months of her life. I'm adapting it slightly, particularly so we can pray it in the first person. Here it is:

> Merciful Father, in the name of our lovable Jesus, the Virgin Mary, and all the Saints, I ask You to set me on fire with Your Spirit of Love and to grant me the grace of making You deeply loved.[177]

I love that prayer. Unfortunately, though, it doesn't count for your consecration day. For that, I'm only giving you two options: Thérèse's actual text or the Prayer of Consecration to Merciful Love.[178] (Of course, you can certainly pray both.) Actually, if you're making the consecration at home with your family, there's one more option. It's called the Family Offering to Merciful Love, and Appendix Two will tell you all about that.

Anyway, whichever prayer you choose for your day of consecration, make sure you spend some time today meditating on it (or on "them," if you decide to pray both prayers tomorrow). And by the way, if you plan to make your consecration in a group setting, see the note at the bottom of page 137. Also, you might want to peek ahead to the second section of tomorrow's reading, "Before Consecration." (Don't worry. It's short.)

Day of Consecration

'The Happy Day'

*B*E *HAPPY.* Congratulations! You've made it to Consecration Day, the day you will offer yourself to Merciful Love, a day of great joy and happiness. As St. Thérèse put it, describing her own day of consecration, "Ah! since the happy day, it seems to me that *Love* penetrates and surrounds me, that at each moment this *Merciful Love* renews me."[179]

Now, my prayer for you is that you also will experience such joy on your consecration day. And why not be joyful? After all, by consecrating yourself to Divine Mercy, you'll be consoling Jesus and making him happy. You'll be receiving all the rejected Merciful Love that other people don't want. You'll be purified by love and, if you live the Little Way and the Offering, you "need have no fear of purgatory."[180] Moreover, your heart will receive healing graces that will make it more sensitive and compassionate to the suffering of others. In other words, your heart will become more like Christ's. Finally, through the grace of such heart healing, you'll become an even more effective channel of God's mercy to others.

So, joy should abound this day! But if it doesn't, if you can't help feeling tired, anxious, or empty — that's perfect. Be happy! What? Let me explain.

The Little Way is not about taking away the dryness of everyday life. (After all, that's part of our "littleness.") Rather, it's about *finding happiness* amid such dryness. It's about discovering extraordinary joy, happiness, and peace in the midst of regular, ordinary, day-to-day existence. Truly, it's the secret to happiness in this life. And I myself can attest to that fact.

For most of my life, I wasn't a very happy person. Let's just say it didn't take much for me to get discouraged and depressed. Well, it was only after I discovered the Little Way and offered myself to Merciful Love more than 15 years ago that I began to experience true peace and joy — a peace and joy that remain with me even to this day. Of course, the joy hasn't always bubbled over, and sometimes I've wavered from the Little Way and lost my peace, but for the most part, it's been a deep and growing peace and joy for 15 years. So, for what it's worth, my own testimony is that the Offering to Merciful Love, the Little

Way of mercy, the rediscovery of the Gospel that St. Thérèse shares with us truly is a formula for happiness — even amid great darkness. But don't just take my word for it.

Before her profession of religious vows, her "wedding day," Thérèse made a retreat. Now, one would think that, in anticipation of such a joyful day, her heart would have been filled with consolation. Instead, everything was dryness and desolation. But that didn't bother her — not in the least. In the following two paragraphs, she explains why and, in the process, reveals the secret of her happiness:

> [The retreat] was far from bringing me any consolations since the most absolute aridity and almost total abandonment were my lot. Jesus was sleeping as usual in my little boat; ah! I see very well how rarely souls allow Him to sleep peacefully within them. Jesus is so fatigued with always having to take the initiative and to attend to others that He hastens to take advantage of the repose I offer to Him. He will undoubtedly awaken before my great eternal retreat, but instead of being troubled about it this only gives me extreme pleasure.
>
> Really, I am far from being a saint, and what I have just said is proof of this; instead of rejoicing, for example, at my aridity, I should attribute it to my little fervor and lack of fidelity; I should be desolate for having slept (for seven years) during my [Holy Hours] and my *thanksgivings* after Holy Communion; well, I am not desolate. I remember that *little children* are as pleasing to their parents when they are asleep as well as when they are wide awake; I remember, too, that when they perform operations, doctors put their patients to sleep. Finally, I remember that: "*The Lord knows our weakness, that he is mindful that we are but dust and ashes.*"[181]

So, as you prepare to consecrate yourself to Merciful Love, if you're feeling happy, then good — be happy! If you are feeling nothing, then good — be happy! Be happy like St. Thérèse, who said of her own dryness, "Instead of being troubled about it, this only gives me extreme pleasure." Be happy like Thérèse, who was "rejoicing" at her "aridity." Be happy like Thérèse, who knew that Jesus loves her, even when he's sleeping (and so, we don't have to constantly prod him for proofs of his love). Be happy like Thérèse, who believed that "He will undoubtedly awaken before my great eternal retreat." Be happy like Thérèse, who, despite feeling "far from being a saint," trusted that God would eventually make her into a great one. Be happy like Thérèse, who knew that good doctors, "when they perform operations, ... put their patients to sleep." In other words, be happy that if you keep living the Little Way, God will especially be working through you even in the midst of your daily darkness and aridity. And, finally, be happy that despite your "little fervor and lack of fidelity," "the Lord knows [your] weakness" and will eventually come down for you and raise you to the heights of his love.

But, of course, we can't just sit back, relax, and enjoy such happiness. We also have to keep trying to grow in holiness. Alright, so let's now express our efforts, our "trying," by getting ready to consecrate ourselves to Merciful Love.

Before Consecration. Okay, now get ready — actually, you already are ready. You've been faithfully preparing for this moment for the last 33 days. So here are just three things I recommend by way of final preparation: (1) If possible, make a good Confession. But if you don't have time to do so before the consecration, then from your heart, tell the Lord you're sorry for your sins, and make a resolution to go to Confession as soon as you reasonably can. (2) Write out or print up the Prayer of Consecration to Merciful Love or Thérèse's own text so you can sign it after you've recited it — if you'd like, you can visit ShopMercy.org for a certificate or prayercard with the Prayer of Consecration to Merciful Love. (3) Get a Divine Mercy Image to put up in your room as a reminder of your consecration — or at least get a small prayercard to put in your wallet or purse.

(See the Resource Pages at the back of this book for more information.) Again, these three things are recommendations. They're not essential to the consecration.

PRAYER OF CONSECRATION. Okay, so you're ready to make your consecration. Now you'll need the right prayer. As I mentioned yesterday, you have two choices (or three choices if you're making the consecration as a family — see Appendix Two). You can either use the Prayer of Consecration to Merciful Love, Thérèse's own Offering to Merciful Love, or both.[182] Whichever you use, I recommend that you recite the prayer after attending Mass or even after receiving Holy Communion (if there's time). If you can't get to Mass, you can still make the consecration. (Mass is highly recommended but not essential.) With or without Mass, after you recite your prayer of consecration, I suggest that you sign it, date it, and keep it in a safe place. (When I renew my consecration annually, I like to recite the prayer from the original copy and then sign and date it again.) Anyway, one more time, here are your two choices:

Prayer of Consecration to Merciful Love

Merciful Father, relying on the prayers and example of Abraham and Mary, my father and mother in faith, and of St. Thérèse, my sister in the way of humble confidence, I, ______________________, choose, this day, with the help of your grace, to strive with all my heart to follow the Little Way. And so,

> I firmly intend to fight discouragement, do little things with great love, and be merciful to my neighbor in deed, word, and prayer.
>
> I aim to keep before my eyes my poverty, weakness, brokenness, and sin, trusting that my littleness and contrite heart will attract your Merciful Love.

> I choose to remain always little, not relying on my own merits but solely on yours, dear Lord, and those of the Blessed Mother.
>
> Finally, I believe, my God, that you can and will make me into a saint, even if I won't see it, even if I have to struggle all my life against vice and sin, even if I have to wait until the very end. This blind hope in your mercy, O Lord, is my only treasure.

And now, to confirm my resolve and to console you for so much rejection of your mercy, I OFFER MYSELF, THROUGH THE HANDS OF MARY IMMACULATE, AS A VICTIM OF HOLOCAUST TO YOUR MERCIFUL LOVE, asking you to consume me incessantly, allowing the waves of *infinite tenderness* shut up within you to overflow into my soul, and that I may thus become a *martyr* of your *love*, O my God, and a gift of mercy to so many others.

I ask all this in Jesus' name. Amen.

Offering to Merciful Love

by St. Thérèse of Lisieux

O My God! Most Blessed Trinity, I desire to *Love* You and make You *Loved*, to work for the glory of Holy Church by saving souls on earth and liberating those suffering in purgatory. I desire to accomplish Your will perfectly and to reach the degree of glory You have prepared for me in Your Kingdom. I desire, in a word, to be a saint, but I feel my helplessness and I beg You, O my God! to be Yourself my *Sanctity*!

Since You loved me so much as to give me Your only Son as my Savior and my Spouse, the infinite treasures of His merits are mine. I offer them to You with gladness, begging You to look upon me only in the Face of Jesus and in His heart burning with *Love*.

I offer You, too, all the merits of the saints (in heaven and on earth), their acts of *Love*, and those of the holy angels. Finally, I offer You, *O Blessed Trinity!* the *Love* and merits of the *Blessed Virgin, my dear Mother*. It is to her I abandon my offering, begging her to present it to You. Her Divine Son, my *Beloved* Spouse, told us in the days of His mortal life: "*Whatsoever you ask the Father in my name he will give it to you!*" I am certain, then, that You will grant my desires; I know, O my God! that *the more You want to give, the more You make us desire*. I feel in my heart immense desires and it is with confidence I ask You to come and take possession of my soul. Ah! I cannot receive Holy Communion as often as I desire, but, Lord, are You not *all-powerful?* Remain in me as in a tabernacle and never separate Yourself from Your little victim.

I want to console You for the ingratitude of the wicked, and I beg of You to take away my freedom to displease You. If through weakness I sometimes fall, may Your *Divine Glance* cleanse my soul immediately, consuming all my imperfections like the fire that transforms everything into itself.

I thank You, O my God! for all the graces You have granted me, especially the grace of making me pass through the crucible of suffering. It is with joy I shall contemplate You on the Last Day carrying the scepter of Your Cross. Since You deigned to give me a share in this very precious Cross, I hope in heaven to resemble You and to see shining in my glorified body the sacred stigmata of Your Passion.

After earth's Exile, I hope to go and enjoy You in the Fatherland, but I do not want to lay up merits for heaven. I want to work for Your *Love alone* with the one purpose of pleasing You, consoling Your Sacred Heart, and saving souls who will love You eternally.

In the evening of this life, I shall appear before You with empty hands, for I do not ask You, Lord, to count my works. All our justice is stained in Your eyes. I wish, then, to be clothed in Your own *Justice* and to receive from Your *Love* the eternal possession of *Yourself.* I want no other *Throne*, no other *Crown* but *You*, my *Beloved!*

Time is nothing in Your eyes, and a single day is like a thousand years. You can, then, in one instant prepare me to appear before You.

In order to live in one single act of perfect Love, I OFFER MYSELF AS A VICTIM OF HOLOCAUST TO YOUR MERCIFUL LOVE, asking You to consume me incessantly, allowing the waves of *infinite tenderness* shut up within You to overflow into my soul, and that thus I may become a *martyr* of Your *Love*, O my God!

May this martyrdom, after having prepared me to appear before You, finally cause me to die and may my soul take its flight without any delay into the eternal embrace of *Your Merciful Love.*

I want, O my *Beloved*, at each beat of my heart to renew this offering to You an infinite number of times, until the shadows having disappeared I may be able to tell You of my *Love* in an *Eternal Face to Face!*[183]

PLEASE NOTE:

If on your day of consecration, you recite your consecration prayer with a group, I highly recommend only using the Prayer of Consecration to Merciful Love. (Then, if you'd like, you can pray St. Thérèse's text of the Offering to Merciful Love on your own.) To obtain a certificate (MLC) or prayercard (33PC) that include the image on the cover of this book and the Prayer of Consecration to Merciful Love, call 800-462-7426 or visit ShopMercy.org. (Please use the above codes when ordering.)

After Consecration
The Lens of Mercy

[Read this section sometime after you've made your consecration. Don't forget!]

So, you've made your consecration to Divine Mercy (your Offering to Merciful Love). Now what? Of course, you're going to want to continue to live the Little Way by doing the three things we learned about on Day 11: (1) *Keep recognizing* the darkness of your littleness and brokenness. (2) *Keep trying* to grow in holiness and do little things with great love. (3) *Keep trusting* and believing that God will satisfy your desires for holiness.

But there's something else. *You'll want to learn to see through the lens of mercy.* Let me begin to explain this by saying something about a seemingly unrelated topic: conscience.

CONSCIENCE. One of the great gifts of the Second Vatican Council is the emphasis it gave to *conscience*, that "voice of God" that speaks to our hearts about loving, doing good, and avoiding evil.[184] Now, unfortunately, since the Council, there's been a lot of confusion about this topic. For instance, while it's true that we should always follow our conscience, sometimes that's all people ever hear about it. But there's more to the story.

Yes, it's true that we should always follow our conscience, *but we also have a responsibility to form our conscience properly.* In other words, what we think is right and wrong may not actually be what's truly right and wrong. In fact, if most of our moral education comes from Hollywood and CNN and not from Sacred Scripture and Church teaching, then we've not formed our consciences properly, and what our conscience tells us will likely be wrong. Now, yes, we would still be obligated to follow our conscience under such circumstances. However, we'd also be guilty of doing wrong because we hadn't taken the time and made the effort to form our conscience properly. So, in a sense, the foundation of the entire moral life comes down to properly forming our conscience.

Alright, so how do we properly form our conscience? Again, we should do it through Scripture and Church teaching. Now, if that sounds like I'm saying we need to roll up our sleeves and begin studying the Bible and the *Catechism of the Catholic Church* — I am. Or we at least need to be properly taught from them. But that's actually where things start to get interesting.

THE FREEDOM OF CONSCIENCE. Did you know that the Church gives us a lot of freedom regarding how we properly form our conscience? Now, of course, it doesn't give us freedom to choose when it comes to something like the Ten Commandments. There, we need to accept all 10, without exception. Still, we do have a lot of freedom regarding how we approach the truths of the moral life, which things we'll emphasize, and which truths we'll especially choose to live by.

We see this kind of freedom, for example, in the saints — particularly in those who gifted the Church with major spiritualities. Take St. Francis of Assisi. Of course, while he certainly embraced all the truths of Scripture and Church teaching, he chose to emphasize *poverty*. That was the lens through which he saw Christ, and so he became poor himself, and poverty colored his walk with Christ.

Francis' choice of poverty affected the way his conscience judged him. In other words, because the ideal of poverty held such a high place in Francis' conscience, his conscience would convict him of sin regarding things that probably wouldn't convict us. For instance, Francis would have certainly felt it sinful for him to accept a family inheritance of a mansion. After all, such a luxury would have gone against his ideal of following the poor Christ, who had "nowhere to lay his head." (Of course, for others, accepting such an inheritance would not necessarily be sinful.)

So, we do have a lot of freedom regarding the way we choose to follow Christ and which truths of the Gospel will loom largest in our heart and conscience. In fact, this freedom of choice is part of the beautiful diversity of the Christian life, and it's something that St. Thérèse very much appreciated. For instance, we read the following in the introduction to her autobiography:

> [Jesus] set before me the book of nature; I understood how all the flowers He has created are beautiful, how the splendor of the rose and the whiteness of the Lily do not take away the perfume of the little violet or the delightful simplicity of the daisy. I understood

> that if all flowers wanted to be roses, nature would lose her springtime beauty, and the fields would no longer be decked out with little wild flowers.
>
> And so it is in the world of souls, Jesus' garden.[185]

So, the diversity of authentic spiritualities within the Church is pleasing to Jesus. But according to St. Thérèse, there's one path that particularly attracts him, one path, more than others, that allows God to manifest "His infinite grandeur": It's the way of mercy. (Or, as Thérèse would put it, it's the "Little Way" of mercy.)

The Way of Mercy. In the same introduction to her autobiography from which we just read, St. Thérèse describes the way of mercy in relation to other paths:

> I understood, too, that Our Lord's love is revealed as perfectly in the most simple soul who resists His grace in nothing as in the most excellent soul; in fact, since the nature of love is to humble oneself, if all souls resembled those of the holy Doctors who illumined the Church with the clarity of their teachings, it seems God would not descend so low when coming to their hearts. But he created the child who knows only how to make his feeble cries heard; He has created the poor savage who has nothing but the natural law to guide him. It is to their hearts that God deigns to lower Himself. These are the wild flowers whose simplicity attracts Him. When coming down in this way, God manifests His infinite grandeur.[186]

Did you catch the revolutionary thinking that's hidden in this passage? It's no less a revolution than the Gospel message that the greatest are the least (see Lk 9:48). It's the idea that *God lowers himself more to give himself to little souls than to the great souls.* And so, "in this way, God manifests His infinite grandeur." In other words, when the Lord stoops down to little souls, it makes his glory shine even more. And that's a big deal.

Look at it like this: From our perspective, the great souls are, well, *the great souls*! They're the important and accomplished people. From God's perspective, though, the truly great souls are the little souls, because they allow God's greatest attribute, his mercy, to shine forth most fully. And if we exist simply to glorify God, then it seems that little souls enable God to manifest his glory even moreso than other souls. After all, "the nature of love is to humble itself." And so, the Little Way is, in a certain sense, the best path for giving God the greatest glory.

Ah, but that's not fair to the big souls! Wrong. Anyone can become a little soul at heart, just as even the materially rich can be poor in spirit. Simply put, the Little Way is a choice. It's a choice that forms our conscience. It's a choice to be little. It's a choice to see ourselves as little. It's a choice to walk the path of spiritual childhood.

Saint Thérèse describes this choice in the following paragraph, which, in my opinion, is the best description of what it means to be a "little soul":

> To remain little is to recognize our nothingness, to expect everything from God (as a little child expects everything from its father; it is to be not too distressed by its faults). *Finally, it is to be worried about nothing, and not to be set on earning our living*. Even among the poor, as long as the child is very little, they give him whatever is necessary; but as soon as he grows up, his father no longer wants to feed him and says: "Work now! You can take care of yourself." Very well, it was so as not to hear this that I never wanted to grow up, feeling that I was incapable of earning *my living, the eternal life of heaven!* (I have always remained little, therefore, having no other occupation but that of gathering flowers, the flowers of love and sacrifice, and of offering them to God in order to please Him. To be little is also to not attribute to oneself the virtues that one practices, believing oneself capable of anything, but to recognize that God places this treasure

of virtue in the hands of His little child, to be used when necessary; but it remains always God's treasure. Finally, it is not to become discouraged over one's faults, for little children fall often, but they are too little to hurt themselves very much.)[187]

These words speak for themselves. So, I will say no more, especially because we've already covered the heart of all this during the retreat, namely, the idea of recognizing our littleness. But here's something we didn't cover earlier, something that pushes us forward along the Little Way as a way of life, something that also forms our conscience: The choice to see through "*the lens of mercy.*"

T*HE* L*ENS OF* M*ERCY*. Just as St. Francis chose to see Christ through the lens of poverty, so St. Thérèse chose to see him and everything else through *the lens of mercy*. She describes this reality in a passage we read earlier, a passage that now deserves a second read:

> *How GOOD is the Lord, his MERCY endures forever!* It seems to me that if all creatures had received the same graces I received, God would be feared by none but would be loved to the point of folly; and through *love*, not through fear, no one would ever consent to cause Him any pain. I understand, however, that all souls cannot be the same, that it is necessary there be different types in order to honor each of God's perfections in a particular way. To me He has granted His *infinite Mercy*, and *through it* I contemplate and adore the other divine perfections! All of these perfections appear to be resplendent *with love*; even His Justice (and perhaps this even more so than the others) seems to me clothed in *love*. What a sweet joy it is to think that God is *Just*, i.e., that He takes into account our weakness, that He is perfectly aware of our fragile nature. What should I fear then?[188]

Again, Thérèse chose to see everything through the lens of mercy. That is the mystery she wanted to glorify, the main mystery that formed her conscience. She chose mercy, and so, "even God's Justice" seemed to her "clothed in *love*." But this was not the kind of justice that Sr. Fébronie sought.

Remember Sr. Fébronie? She was the subprioress in the Lisieux convent who thought Thérèse was being presumptuous when she taught others to trust boldly in God's mercy so as to avoid the punishment of purgatory. In other words, Fébronie was perhaps like the "sons of thunder" in the Gospel, who wanted punishment and strict justice for sinners (see Lk 9:54). She was perhaps like some of us who see sins in the Church and the world, get angry, and want fire and brimstone to come down. Well, an exasperated St. Thérèse said to Sr. Fébronie (and, perhaps, to us, too): "*My sister, if you look for the justice of God you will get it.*" And Sr. Fébronie got it. According to Thérèse, she went to purgatory, where she was "delivered up to the full justice of God," which doesn't sound very comforting.

So, we have a choice: severe justice or tender mercy. Now, I don't know about you, but I choose mercy! I choose to see through the lens of mercy. So, what about you? What do you choose? Before you answer, I should repeat what we learned on Day 19, namely, that mercy is a double-edged sword. I say that because, as Scripture teaches, the measure with which we measure will be measured back to us (see Lk 6:38). So, to choose the path of mercy is also to choose to *be* merciful. After all, only the merciful will be shown mercy (see Mt 5:7, 18:21-35). So, if you want God to be strict with everyone, and if you yourself decide to be strict with others, *then God will be strict with you.* Again, I don't know about you, but I choose mercy and hope to live mercy. But what about you? What do you choose?

THE WORK OF MERCY. If you decide to choose mercy, that's great! But know that your decision is going to cost you some work. I mean, proper conscience formation and learning to see through the lens of mercy doesn't just happen. It takes effort. Okay, so what do you need to do? Well, I have three recommendations.

1. Read the Mercy Saints. My first recommendation is to read books about mercy from people who have chosen the path of mercy, who have done the "work of mercy," and who saw through the lens of mercy. Now, first and foremost, in my opinion, would be to read the autobiography of St. Thérèse of Lisieux, called *Story of a Soul.*[189] But please don't get distracted by the sometimes flowery language. It's a masterpiece, especially the later chapters.

Second, I recommend the spiritual journal of St. Faustina, *Divine Mercy in My Soul: Diary of Saint Maria Faustina Kowalska.* Like Thérèse, Faustina also chose to see everything through the lens of mercy.[190] In fact, the two saints are amazingly similar in their message and, in my opinion, are the best guides for helping people to see everything through a lens of mercy. They truly are the great apostles of mercy for our time. (For other recommended titles on mercy, see the Resource Pages.)

2. Get an Image of Divine Mercy. They say a picture is worth a thousand words, and the Image of Divine Mercy is a thousand words of mercy. Knowing that we all have a distorted image of God as a result of original sin (see Day 1), Jesus wants to heal that distortion by giving us a true image of his mercy for our time. Specifically, he appeared to St. Faustina and told her to paint an image of himself with the words "Jesus, I trust in you" at the bottom. He promised to give great graces through the image,[191] and it's become a source of healing for tens of millions of people throughout the world. I can think of no better way to begin to see through the lens of mercy than by spending time each day gazing upon this image of Jesus.

Now, while Jesus' promise of grace applies to every Image of Divine Mercy,[192] I highly recommend the recently restored "Vilnius" version (see above, center), which is the original image painted under St. Faustina's careful direction. (See the Resource Pages for more information.) Also, if you do get an Image of Divine Mercy, you may want to consider enthroning it in your home. (See Appendix Two for more information.)

3. Become a Marian Missionary of Divine Mercy. The Marian Missionaries of Divine Mercy (MMDM) is for people who *really* want to get into mercy as a spirituality. It's basically an organization for those who complete a thorough adult-faith formation program that goes through all aspects of a Divine Mercy spirituality. That program is called *Hearts Afire: Parish-based Programs from the Marian Fathers of the Immaculate Conception* (HAPP®), and you can learn more about it in the Resource Pages.

After completing HAPP, belonging to the MMDM organization as a Marian Missionary involves a minimal commitment of prayer and service, and includes opportunities for further formation from myself and our Divine Mercy team at the National Shrine of the Divine Mercy in Stockbridge, Massachusetts.

If you think you might be interested in becoming a Marian Missionary, you can order the free MMDM handbook, which is the official manual for Marian Missionaries and explains everything. Visit MarianMissionaries.org or see the Resource Pages for more information.

CLOSING PRAYER. I hope you'll find these three recommendations helpful for learning to see through the lens of mercy. Now, may I ask you to pray for me, my community (The Marian Fathers of the Immaculate Conception), and all the Marian Missionaries of Divine Mercy? Specifically, would you pray the following prayer of St. Thérèse for us?

> Merciful Father, in the name of our lovable Jesus, the Virgin Mary, and all the Saints, I ask You to set the Marian Fathers and the Marian Missionaries of Divine Mercy on fire with Your Spirit of Love and to grant them the grace of making You deeply loved.[193]

Thank you for your prayers. I will also pray this prayer for you, and I hope you enjoyed your retreat. May your Offering to Merciful Love (your consecration to Divine Mercy) bring you great gifts of happiness, peace, and joy. God bless you. +

APPENDIX ONE
Living the Offering

In the text of her Offering to Merciful Love, St. Thérèse talks about her desire to "console" Jesus, to live in "one single act of perfect love," and to renew her Offering with "each beat" of her heart. But what does all this mean? How can we *console Jesus*? How does the Offering allow us to live "*in one single act of perfect love*"? And how could one renew the Offering *with each beat of his or her heart*?

I've often pondered these questions, and what follows are three answers that, I hope, will help us live the Offering to Merciful Love with the same generous spirit as the Saint of Lisieux.

How We Can Console Jesus

Saint Thérèse frequently wrote about her desire to console Jesus, and as we learned on Day 20, that was her main motivation in making the Offering to Merciful Love. However, the idea of "consoling Jesus" (the Head of his body)[194] sometimes causes difficulties for people. For instance, they'll say things like this:

> How can I console Jesus when he's happy in heaven? I mean, it seems that Jesus is the one who needs to console *me*, not the other way around. After all, while he's joyfully reigning on high in his resurrected glory, I still have to trod along in this valley of tears.

To address such difficulties, I dedicated a whole section of the book *Consoling the Heart of Jesus* to the question, "How can I console Jesus if he's happy in heaven?[195] Since that time, however, I've reflected even more deeply on this topic, and here I'd like to share some insights that both complement that earlier writing and help summarize the theology of consoling the Heart of Jesus (in three points).

1. God Doesn't Need Us. Let's be clear about something right off the bat: God doesn't need us. He's perfectly happy in and of himself. As Father, Son, and Holy Spirit, he's a perfect Family of Love, and we can add nothing to his greatness, glory, or happiness.

Now, on this topic of "God not needing us," I'd say that Exodus 3:14 puts it best. That's where God spoke to Moses from the burning bush and revealed his name as "I AM." At that moment, he seemed to be telling us: "Look, I AM — and *you're not.* I created you and hold you in existence. Without me, you are *nothing.* I am completely self-sufficient and don't need you, but you need me for *everything.*"

Alright, so we acknowledge that God is completely self-sufficient and content. He doesn't need us. However, at this point, perhaps some of us are experiencing at least something of St. Faustina Kowalska's own sentiments:

> It seems to me as though Jesus could not be happy without me, nor could I, without Him. Although I understand that, being God, He is happy in Himself and has absolutely no need of any creature, still, His goodness compels Him to give Himself to the creature, and with a generosity which is beyond understanding.[196] … I do not know how to live without God, but I also feel that God, absolutely self-sufficient though He is, cannot be happy without me.[197]

So, let's now consider this "generosity which is beyond understanding" and how God, "absolutely self-sufficient though He is," in a sense, "cannot be happy" without *us.*

2. The Word Became Flesh. Although God does not need us, he chose to become one of us out of love: "God so loved the world that he gave his only begotten Son" (Jn 3:16). And when the Son became incarnate, when the Word became flesh, he became "like us in all things but sin."[198] Alright, but what gets to the essence of what he became? In other words, what's most characteristic of humanity?

Well, if you were to ask the philosophers, most of them would probably say, "It's *reason* — that's what separates us from the animals. That's what makes us who we are." However, if you were to ask the writers of Sacred Scripture, they'd say there's something even more characteristic of humanity than reason, namely, *the heart.*[199] Indeed, they'd say that the heart gets to the very center of man and to what's most important about him. (This is probably why we don't see in our churches statues of "the Sacred Brain of Jesus" but, rather, statues of *his Sacred Heart.*)

So, at the incarnation, Jesus, the eternal Son, assumed a human nature and *a human heart.*[200] And if his Heart truly is human, if he truly is like us in all things but sin, then his Heart is filled with the desire not only to love but also *to be loved.* (After all, how could someone be fully human without desiring to be loved?) In other words, by taking on a human heart, God, in Christ, *made himself vulnerable.* Not by necessity but by his free choice, God allowed himself, in Jesus Christ, to feel a *need* for our love.

Think of it: The One who doesn't need us decided to make himself need us! And so, this vulnerability of God in Christ is part of the "poverty of the incarnation" (see 2 Cor 8:9) and is a particularly profound aspect of the "self-emptying" of Jesus, who, "though he was in the form of God … did not deem equality with God something to be grasped at" (Phil 2:6-7). And because the human heart of Jesus is united to and burns with Divine Love, his desire to love and *to be loved* infinitely surpasses our own desires. In fact, you might say that the self-revelation of God through the burning bush as "I AM" advances to the self-revelation of God through the burning love of the Cross as "*I thirst*" (Jn 19:28).

"I thirst." Those words express it best.[201] Indeed, Jesus feels not just a desire but a *burning thirst* for love from those for whom he gave up his life. Moreover, by striving to quench his thirst for love, by loving him in return, we have mercy on him. We console him.

Saint John Paul II expressed the theology of consoling Jesus in what is probably the most profound papal statement on the topic. And while he doesn't specifically use the term "console,"[202] it's clear that that's what he's getting at:

> The events of Good Friday and, even before that, in prayer in Gethsemane, introduce a fundamental change into the whole course of the revelation of love

> and mercy in the messianic mission of Christ. The one who "went about doing good and healing" and "curing every sickness and disease" now Himself seems to merit the greatest mercy and to *appeal for mercy*, when He is arrested, abused, condemned, scourged, crowned with thorns, when He is nailed to the cross and dies amidst agonizing torments. It is then that He particularly deserves mercy from the people to whom He has done good, and He does not receive it ... .
>
> [T]he cross will remain the point of reference for other words too of the Revelation of John: "Behold, I stand at the door and knock; if anyone hears my voice and opens the door, I will come in and eat with him and he with me." In a special way, God also reveals His mercy when He invites man to have "mercy" on His only Son, the crucified one.
>
> ... Christ, precisely as the crucified one, is the Word that does not pass away, and He is the one who stands at the door and knocks at the heart of every man, without restricting his freedom, but instead seeking to draw from this very freedom love, which is not only an act of solidarity with the suffering Son of man, but also a kind of "mercy" shown by each one of us to the Son of the eternal Father. In the whole of this messianic program of Christ, in the whole revelation of mercy through the cross, could man's dignity be more highly respected and ennobled, for, in obtaining mercy, he is in a sense the one who at the same time "shows mercy"?[203]

So, what's the word of Christ "that does not pass away"? What's the word he speaks as he "knocks at the heart of every man"? Again, I suggest it's his words, "I thirst," spoken from the Cross. And those words "do not pass away" because they were spoken by the Word Incarnate, who is the same "yesterday, today, and forever" (Heb 13:8). Indeed, those are words that, as the *Catechism* says, "cannot remain only in the past," words that "participate in the divine eternity," words that "transcend all times while being made present in them all," words that "abide."[204] In fact, those words — "I thirst" — are directed to each one of us. After all, we know that as he suffered on the Cross, the God-Man "knew and loved us each and all."[205]

But why? Why did God make himself vulnerable in that way? Why did he put himself in "need" of mercy from us? And why, as John Paul II put it, does doing so "highly respect" us and "ennoble" us? We'll answer all this in the next point.

3. He Calls Us "Friends." God made himself vulnerable in Jesus Christ — he put himself in need of our love and mercy — *for the sake of friendship.* In fact, in the very Gospel that records Jesus saying, "I thirst" from the Cross, on the very night he entered into his Passion, Jesus says to us, "No longer do I call you slaves ... but I have called you friends" (Jn 15:15). It's really all about friendship. And as Aristotle rightly pointed out long ago, true friendship requires a kind of equality and mutuality — it can't be one-sided.[206]

So, let me ask you: Have you ever had a friendship where you shared with your friend but he or she never shared with you? (Or maybe it was the other way around.) Of course not! That's not friendship. That seems more like a pastoral or clinical relationship. But true friendship is a two-way street. True friends help one another, are in need of each other, and share their joys and sorrows, hopes and concerns.

But how can we have a true friendship with Jesus if it's just a one-way street? How can we have a deep, personal relationship with him if we're the only ones suffering? How can it be true friendship if we're the only ones in need? On that latter point, Karol Wojtyla (the future St. John Paul II) went so far as to say, "After many experiences and a lot of thinking, I am convinced that *the objective starting point of love is the realization that I am needed by another.*"[207] He goes on to call this reality "a fragment of life's deep logic."[208] But if Jesus doesn't need us, then how can there be a true and loving friendship between him and us?

As we learned in point one, the eternal God, in his divinity, doesn't need us. However, as we learned in point two, *for the sake of friendship*, in Jesus Christ, the incarnate Son of God chose to need our love. And because he needs our love, because his Heart experiences both joys and sorrows, we can enter into true friendship with him. So, he can share with us not only his joys *but also his needs, sorrows, and pains* — and we can console him.

But how do we console him? We console him by loving him, letting him love us, and by allowing him to have mercy on us and save us. In fact, that's really the most amazing part: Jesus' "need" is to show mercy and to save us. And when people reject his mercy, when they reject his gift of salvation, it causes him pain. But when they let him love them and let him have mercy on them (such as by making the Offering to Merciful Love), they, thereby, console him.

So we help Jesus by letting him help us! That's what John Paul II marvels at when he asks, "Could man's dignity be more highly respected and ennobled, for, in obtaining mercy, [man] is in a sense the one who at the same time 'shows mercy'?"

In sum then: God doesn't need us, but in Christ Jesus, he chose to need our love. And he chose to feel that need for the sake of friendship, which is a two-way street. In other words, our acceptance of Christ's gift of mercy and salvation is also *a gift that we give to him*. Think of it. It's truly amazing. God gives us the dignity of having mercy on Jesus *by letting him have mercy on us!*[209]

Now, on to the answer to the second question.

How to Live in "One Single Act of Perfect Love"

What does St. Thérèse mean when she says she wants to live in "one single act of perfect love"? In one sense, I think she means that she wants God himself to love in and through her with his own love, which is perfect. (Thus, she says in the text of the Offering that she wants God himself to be her "Sanctity" and wants God to look upon her "only in the Face of Jesus and in His Heart burning with *Love*.") So, in this sense, the perfection is on *God's side*. Okay, but in another sense, I think it could have something to do with perfection on *our side*. Let me explain.

To understand what I mean by perfection "on our side," it will be helpful to look at what the Church means by "perfect contrition." Perfect contrition is when we're sorry for our sins not because we fear hell and punishment but, rather, *because our sins offend God, whom we love.* (Imperfect contrition, on the other hand, is sorrow for sin because of fear of hell and punishment.) So, the key element of what the Church calls "perfect" contrition is that it's motivated by love for God and a desire not to offend him or let him down.

Well, I think we can live, so to speak, in "one act of perfect love" if our central motivation in life is like that of perfect contrition. In other words, I would describe such "perfect love of God" as our being motivated to serve God not because we're seeking merits and the rewards of heaven but, rather, simply because *we love God and want to please him and console him.* (Imperfect love of God would have to do with a desire for reward.)

In view of all this, it's not surprising that, in the Offering to Merciful Love, Thérèse highlights the contrast between what I'm calling "perfect love of God" and "imperfect love of God." For instance, she says, "I do not want to lay up merits for heaven. I want to work for Your *Love alone* with the one purpose of pleasing You, consoling Your Sacred Heart." The "merits" language has to do with the reward of heaven (imperfect love). The "pleasing" and "consoling" language has to do with a desire simply to love God for who he is (perfect love).

Okay, but how does one live this perfect motivation as a *single act* of one's life? I suggest that the answer comes from what we learned on Day 6 of this retreat. There, we read that "it's all about consoling Jesus." In other words, it's all about loving Jesus with "perfect love," the kind of love where we don't seek to console ourselves but, rather, seek to console him. And how do we console him best? Inspired by the *Diary* of St. Faustina, I said it's to *trust* in him. And what does trust in Jesus mean? According to Fr. Seraphim, it means "praise and thanksgiving." It means to praise and thank God in all things.

Now, Fr. Seraphim's answer is very interesting. It's like this: Is trust an act of love? Not necessarily. I say that because you can trust your doctor without loving him. However, if you trust in Jesus *for the purpose of consoling him, then trust becomes an act of love.* In fact, it becomes *an act of perfect love*, because perfect love, like perfect contrition, is concerned with the Lord's Heart. It seeks to please him and console him.

Alright, so how do we live that act of perfect love always as "one act"? I suggest that we can do so by living our lives *with the one purpose of consoling Jesus through our attitude of trust, which means praising and thanking God in all things and in all circumstances.* If we can do that, then we'll be living in one single act of perfect love, like St. Thérèse — *and St. Faustina.* Yes, Faustina lived this way as well, and I'd like to now conclude this section with a passage from her *Diary* that summarizes this attitude of perfect love:

> I know that I am under Your special gaze, O Lord. I do not examine with fear Your plans regarding me; my task is to accept everything from Your hand. I do not fear anything, although the storm is raging, and frightful bolts strike all around me, and I then feel quite alone. Yet, my heart senses You, and my trust grows, and I see all Your omnipotence which upholds me. *With You, Jesus, I go through life, amid storms and rainbows, with a cry of joy, singing the song of Your mercy. I will not stop singing my song of love until the choir of Angels picks it up.* There is no power that can stop me in my flight toward God.[210]

How to Renew the Offering with Every Breath: The Spiritual Communion of Merciful Love

[The following is adapted from *Consoling the Heart of Jesus* by Fr. Michael Gaitley, MIC.]

Okay, so I haven't yet figured out how to renew the Offering to Merciful Love with every beat of the heart. However, I can suggest a way of renewing it with every breath. It's called the Spiritual Communion of Merciful Love. Now, before I explain what it is, I should first say something about spiritual communions in general.

So, what's a spiritual communion? It basically consists of making a prayer of desire to receive Jesus in Holy Communion. For instance, one can simply pray: "Lord Jesus, I long to receive you in Holy Communion, but because I can't do so now, I ask you to come into my heart through spiritual communion." According to one of the greatest theologians in the Church, St. Thomas Aquinas, this kind of prayer can be amazingly powerful. He wrote that a person who fervently makes such a prayer of spiritual communion can receive the same grace as one who fervently receives sacramental Communion![211] Alright, so now that we know what it is and its potential power, let's see how we can make the Spiritual Communion of Merciful Love.

The Spiritual Communion of Merciful Love is a special communion with a particular emphasis. Specifically, it's to console Jesus by making a spiritual communion with the intention of receiving the mercy that other people reject. In other words, it's to see the Eucharist (even spiritually received) as a channel through which Jesus can pour out on us the superabundance of his rejected mercy.

Great! But how, specifically, can we make it? Well, it's as simple as breathing — sort of. Let me explain.

Think of your breathing: in/out — in/out — in/out. Now, notice that after exhaling (out), for a brief moment, before the next inhale (in), your lungs are empty: empty/in/out — empty/in/out — empty/in/out. Before we go further into those three moments of breathing, let me say something about three words from Scripture.

MARY'S THREE WORDS. The three words from Scripture, in Latin, are as follows: *ecce, fiat, magnificat.* Each of these words was spoken by Mary, and each word following the other is a way of continually making a spiritual communion of Merciful Love with the Heart of Mary.

The Latin word *ecce* means "behold." Mary spoke this word at the Annunciation when the angel Gabriel announced to her that she would be the mother of the Messiah. Mary said, "Behold (*Ecce*), I am the handmaid of the Lord" (Lk 1:38). In other words, she presented herself to the Lord just as she was.

When we pray, God wants us to present ourselves to him as we are, like Mary did. He wants us to say, "*Ecce*," that is, "Behold, here I am, O Lord." Yet there's obviously a big difference between Mary and us: We sin; Mary never sinned. Does this fact mean we're unacceptable to the Lord? Absolutely not. Quite the contrary, in fact.

Sometimes we may be tempted to avoid going to Jesus because of our weaknesses, sinfulness, and attachments. This is the temptation of Jansenist fear, but there's no need to be afraid. We console Jesus' Heart when we go to him just as we are — it breaks his Heart when we don't. We don't have to be perfect to go to him. In fact, the weaker and more sinful we are, the more he wants us to go to him and present ourselves with complete honesty and truth: "*Ecce* ... behold, Lord, here I am, sinfulness and all." If only we would always remember how much this pleases him! May we not be afraid to pray, "*Ecce*, here I am, O Lord." May we not give in to the lie that says we're ugly to the Lord. We are not. We're so beautiful to him just as we are. In fact, his Merciful Heart is particularly attracted to the weakest, most sinful souls. My explanation of the next word will say more about this.

The Latin word *fiat* comes from *Fiat mihi*, "Let it be done to me." At the Annunciation, Mary spoke this word after she presented herself to the Lord (*ecce*). Jesus also wants us to speak this word, *fiat*, after we present ourselves to him. Yet, when we speak it, it has a bit of a different meaning than Mary's *fiat*. When Mary said, "Let it be done to me," she was allowing the Incarnation of the Word to take place in her immaculate soul. When we say, "Let it be done to me," we're allowing God's Merciful Love to come pouring down into our weak, sinful souls.

It might be helpful to think of our *fiat* in the following way. First, imagine that the heavens above are an infinite ocean. Next, imagine that this ocean is held back from emptying out onto the earth by a giant floodgate. Well, when we say "*fiat*," it's the magic word that unlocks the gate, and once this gate is unlocked, look out! The waters of the heavenly ocean burst through and pour down into our souls like a great cascading waterfall. But don't be afraid, for as we'll now see, this ocean is a wonderful thing to experience.

As you might have guessed, the ocean I just described is the ocean of God's Merciful Love. Now, Merciful Love is that particular kind of love that seeks out brokenness, suffering, sin, and weakness. Do we understand, then, why Jesus loves it when we go to him as we are, sinfulness and all? It's because weakness and wretchedness are precisely what attracts his Merciful Love. Thus, he simply (and eagerly) awaits our *fiat*. When we give it, look out! We get washed in the wonderful flood of his Merciful Love. Now, let's turn to the third word spoken by Mary.

The word *magnificat* comes from Mary's exclamation in Latin, *Magnificat anima mea Dominum*, "My soul magnifies the Lord." This is Mary's song of praise when she went to her cousin Elizabeth after giving her *fiat* to the Lord (see Lk 1:46-55). Mary was full of praise because of the "great things" God had done for her. After our *fiat*, after we've experienced the power of God's Merciful Love, we, too, will want to give praise to God. We, too, will want to sing out, "*Magnificat!*"

In the last section on "one act of perfect love," I pointed out that the best way to console the Heart of Jesus is to trust him. I also said, thanks to Fr. Seraphim, that the concrete expression of that trust is praise and thanksgiving. Well, because *magnificat* basically means the same as praise and thanksgiving, when we give our *magnificat* to the Lord, we're consoling him in the "best possible way." Of course, sometimes it's easier to praise and thank the Lord than at other times. Moreover, sometimes our praise will have no outward expression at all. It'll just be an act of the will in the depths of our hearts — and that's just fine with Jesus. We give him what we can, and he's happy with that. Nonetheless, when we consider the Merciful Love that God pours into our hearts, it tends to be much easier to let out an outward song of praise.

Having explained the meaning of the three words *ecce*, *fiat*, and *magnificat*, now I'm going to apply them to the three moments of our breathing: empty, in, and out.

Mary's Words Applied to Breathing. Recall that one of the moments of breathing is called "empty." It's that brief, fragile moment in between an exhale and an inhale that, if we were to hold it too long, we might pass out. Well, that moment of emptiness illustrates for us our utter *ecce*. In other words, it shows us what we are of our own sinful selves: empty, weak, and on the verge of passing out. In fact, we can only remain in the moment of "empty lungs" for a short time before we pass out and die. This is exactly what we are at *ecce*. We're saying, "Behold, Lord, here I am — without your mercy, I'll collapse and die." Of course, when we present ourselves to the Lord like that, he rushes to us with his mercy, and we take a deep breath in.

The moment "in" obviously refers to inhale and follows the moment of empty lungs. This moment "in" feels great, especially if we've held empty lungs for 10 to 20 seconds. Go ahead. Try it. Inhale after doing about 20 seconds of empty lungs. Doesn't the inflow of air feel great? Savor it for a moment before you let it go. Hold it for a few moments and enjoy.

What you've just experienced (inhaling) illustrates what happens when we say "*fiat*." For, when we say it, we allow God's Merciful Love to flow into our hearts, and it feels great. It's exactly what we need, namely, his mercy entering into our emptiness. Breathe it in.

Now realize this: Each inhale can be a spiritual communion. It becomes one if we make it our intention when we inhale to receive God's rejected Merciful Love into our emptiness. It's especially like receiving sacramental Communion if we imagine that the Merciful Love we inhale is coming down from the pierced side of Christ as blood and water. (More on this later.)

Obviously, after we inhale, we'll need to blow the air back out (exhale). This is the "out" moment of breathing. Similarly, after we "inhale" God's Merciful Love, because it was so good and refreshing, we'll "need" to praise and thank him for the gift of his mercy. This praise and thanks is signified by the air we exhale from our lungs. We give it back to God as an exhaled *magnificat*.

Okay, having explained the meaning of *ecce*, *fiat*, and *magnificat* and how each of these three words applies to the three moments of our breathing (*ecce*/empty, *fiat*/in, *magnificat*/out), I think it might be helpful to put it all together with a meditation. After all, if we live this breathing exercise as a prayer, then we can constantly be making a spiritual communion, renewing the Offering to Merciful Love, and living praise and thanks. To make our meditation, let's go to the foot of the Cross just before Jesus dies.

Breathing Meditation. Almost everyone else has abandoned him, but Mary is here with you. She puts her words on your lips, "*Ecce* ... Here I am, Lord." You continue: "Here I am, Lord, with all my sinfulness, weaknesses, and attachments. I don't deserve to be here, but I've learned this pleases you. So, behold, O Lord, I come here to console you, even as you are about to die." This humble confidence consoles Jesus right at the moment he breathes his last.

As you pause here in the *ecce* moment with empty lungs, the soldier's lance thrusts through Jesus' side and into his Heart, causing blood and water to flow out and down like a waterfall, down into your heart and soul. As the first drops of this blood and water touch your face, you take a deep breath in, *fiat*. This blood and water (which is his mercy) and this wonderful air (which is also his mercy) fill your soul. After your soul has filled, after your lungs have filled, you linger at the end of the *fiat* moment as you simply enjoy and take delight in his Merciful Love.

Ah, but after having rested for a brief time in the *fiat* moment, your heart and lungs are ready to release what you've just enjoyed. You're ready to breathe back out to the Lord your love and mercy, your praise and thanks. And so, although he seems to be dead (because this is a meditation, you actually still console him), Mary gently raises you to his lips. You breathe into him your praise and thanks, the love and mercy that his blood and water have given you. In this *magnificat* moment, Jesus' lungs slowly fill with your praise and thanks. Yet his Heart can't hold this returned love, for it's been pierced, and now your lungs are empty. Don't worry. Mary gently lowers you to the foot of the Cross, where the blood and water again begin to flow down from the Lord's pierced side and into your emptiness, into the poverty of your *ecce*. And so begins again that wonderful cycle of love and mercy: *ecce*/empty — *fiat*/in — *magnificat*/out — *ecce*/empty — *fiat*/in — *magnificat*/out.

If we live this attitude of presenting our wretchedness to the Lord (*ecce*), receiving his mercy (*fiat*), and then praising and thanking him for his saving mercy (*magnificat*), we can be assured that we won't seriously be wounding the Lord by our lack of trust — for trust is not only praise and thanks, it's also to receive God's mercy. Remember how Fr. Seraphim said that to live trust means to praise and thank God for everything? Some people might have read that and thought, "Hmmm. That's all well and good, but I don't always feel full of praise and thanks, especially when it's hard to be grateful because of life's hurts." Isn't that the truth? But look at what we've just learned from the *ecce*, *fiat*, *magnificat* movement: The path to praise begins with the *ecce* moment. Moreover, while we're in the *ecce* moment, we normally don't feel like praising and thanking, and that's all right. For, from the *ecce* moment, we eventually move to the *fiat* moment. That is, we call down (*fiat*) the Lord's blood and water (mercy) into our emptiness. Then, that *fiat* moment eventually leads to *magnificat*, to praise and thanks.

Don't worry if you're in the *ecce* moment for a long time. For the simple act of presenting yourself to the Lord as you are, sinfulness and all, is itself an act of trust. Furthermore, the act of receiving God's Merciful Love (*fiat*) is also an act of trust, and both these acts of trust (*ecce* and *fiat*) tend to lead to a further act of trust, namely, praise and thanks (*magnificat*).

So, there you have a way to live the Offering to Merciful Love and renew it with every breath as a spiritual communion of Merciful Love.

Appendix Two

Family Offering and Divine Mercy Image Enthronement

[This appendix is an excerpt from *Divine Mercy Image Explained* by Fr. Michael Gaitley, MIC.]

One of the great blessings of being a priest is that I get to live in the same house as the Blessed Sacrament. Because of this, many of my lay friends have expressed a "holy envy" of me, saying they wish they could also live so close to the Eucharist. I try to console them by inviting them to get an Image of Divine Mercy, which, in my opinion, is "the next best thing." I say that because, while the Divine Mercy Image is certainly not a Sacrament, it is an extraordinary image of grace.[212]

Actually, I tell my friends not just to get a Divine Mercy Image for their homes but to *enthrone* it in their homes. In other words, I encourage them, with their families, to solemnly invite Jesus, the King of Mercy, to reign in their homes and then to use the image as a sign, symbol, and reminder of this invitation. Those who have done so are amazed at how powerfully Jesus takes them up on their offer. He truly comes to visit them with a superabundance of his mercy!

In what follows, I'd like to say more about this invitation to Jesus, the Divine Mercy, explain how to make it, and then describe how to enthrone the image.

An Invitation to Jesus, the Divine Mercy. There are lots of reasons why people invite others into their homes. Perhaps it's to have a business meeting, a celebration, or simply to get the furnace fixed. Of course, it's also possible to invite someone into our homes as an act of mercy. For example, I once spent a year studying in a foreign country and had nowhere to go for Christmas. One of my teachers felt sorry for me and graciously invited me to spend Christmas with her and her family — a true act of mercy!

Well, what I mean by solemnly inviting Jesus, the Divine Mercy, into our homes is somewhat similar. It's basically where we turn to the Lord and, feeling sorry for him, invite him to come in. Now, that may sound silly, at least until we realize that the idea for it comes from an important Divine Mercy saint and Doctor of the Church, St. Thérèse of Lisieux.

Because Jesus was so moved by St. Thérèse's ardent love for him, he gave her a beautiful insight into the mystery of his Heart. Specifically, he revealed to her that his Heart suffers terrible pain because he longs to pour out his mercy on souls, but so many refuse to receive it. This rejection of his love, Thérèse learned, is one of the deepest pains of his Heart. Upon realizing this, Thérèse was moved to such a profound compassion for Jesus that, for the purpose of consoling his Heart, she invited him to give her all the mercy that other souls reject. This invitation pleased Jesus so much that he filled her with a superabundance of his mercy, and the experience of it became the very center of Thérèse's whole spirituality, leading her to the heights of holiness.

Alright, that's great for St. Thérèse, but what does it have to do with our topic? Actually, a lot. I say that because Jesus doesn't just want to pour out his rejected Merciful Love on individuals, like St. Thérèse. I believe, he also and especially wants to pour out his mercy on *families*. Why? Because in our day, when the family is so much under attack and when, sadly, so many families refuse God's mercy, Jesus' Heart is especially wounded. Therefore, he's looking for families who will invite him into their homes and allow him to give them the love that so many other families reject. He's looking for families who want to receive his gifts of mercy, love, peace, and joy. In short, he's looking for families to make a Family Offering to Merciful Love. What about your family?[213]

In the next section, I'll explain how you and your family can invite Jesus, the Divine Mercy, into your home and, then, how you can enthrone the Image of Divine Mercy there as well.

How to Make the Invitation (Offering). Making the Family Offering to Merciful Love is rather simple. First, for the purpose of consoling the Heart of Jesus, invite the Lord to give you and your family the mercy that other families reject. Then, each member of your family should strive to accept this rejected mercy and share it with others.[214] It's that simple. Also, don't worry if your family is not perfect. In fact, it's perfect if you're not perfect! After all, Jesus said, "The greater the sinner, the greater the right he has to My mercy."[215] Well, these words also apply to families, so one could say, "The more sinful the family, the more right it has to God's mercy." So, no matter how much a family struggles with sin, the members can still make the Family Offering to Merciful Love. They simply need to try sincerely to turn away from sin, invite the Lord into their home, and receive and share his Merciful Love.

I suggest the following formula for making a Family Offering to Merciful Love, which begins with Jesus' words to St. Faustina, who, like St. Thérèse, lived this spirituality to the full:

> **LEADER:** Jesus, you said to St. Faustina: "The flames of mercy are burning me. I desire to pour them out upon human souls. Oh, what pain they cause Me when they do not want to accept them![216] You, at least, come to Me as often as possible and take these graces they do not want to accept. In this way you will console My Heart. Oh, how indifferent are souls to so much goodness, to so many proofs of love! My Heart drinks only of the ingratitude and forgetfulness of souls living in the world. They have time for everything, but they have no time to come to Me for graces.[217] My daughter, take the graces that others spurn; take as many as you can carry.[218] I want to give myself to souls and to fill them with My love, but few there are who want to accept all the graces My love has intended for them. My grace is not lost; if the soul for whom it was intended does not accept it, another soul takes it."[219]
>
> **ALL:** Lord Jesus, if you want to pour out your mercy on souls, how much more must you desire to pour it out on whole families, especially in our time when so many families reject you. Therefore, Jesus, we the ______________________ Family, offer ourselves to your Merciful Love and ask for the grace and mercy

that other families refuse. We ask this so as to console your Heart and because we need your mercy. Fill us with your mercy, Lord. Please forgive us our sins. We're sorry for our sins, and we ask for the grace to be merciful to one another in our deeds, words, and prayers.

Merciful Savior, may the rays of mercy that go forth from your Heart reign in our home and in our hearts. Please make our home a place where your mercy can rest and where we, too, can find rest in your mercy. Bless us with your mercy when we leave our home and bless us again when we return. Bless everyone we meet with the mercy you pour into our hearts. Especially bless those who visit our home — may they experience your mercy here.

Mary, Our Mother of Mercy, help us to faithfully live our Offering to God's Merciful Love. We give ourselves to you and ask you to share with us your Immaculate Heart. Help us to accept your Son's mercy with your own openness of heart at the Annunciation. Help us to be grateful for God's mercy with your own joyfulness of heart at the Visitation. Help us to trust in God's mercy, especially during times of darkness, with your own steadfast faith at Calvary. Finally, Mary, protect and preserve our family in love, so that one day, we may rejoice together with you and all the saints in the communion of the eternal Family of Love — Father, Son, and Holy Spirit. Amen.

L: St. Joseph, **A:** Pray for us.
L: St. Faustina, **A:** Pray for us.
L: St. Thérèse, **A:** Pray for us.

I recommend that a family make such an offering (or renew it) on one of their favorite Marian feasts, on St. Joseph's feast day (March 19), or on one of the "Mercy feasts" such as the memorial of St. Thérèse of Lisieux (Oct. 1), the memorial of St. Faustina

(Oct. 5), Divine Mercy Sunday (the Second Sunday of Easter),[220] or Trinity Sunday, which is the day St. Thérèse first received the inspiration to offer herself to Merciful Love. (See chart on pages 22-23 for other recommended feast days.)

DIVINE MERCY IMAGE ENTHRONEMENT. The Divine Mercy Image goes perfectly with the Family Offering to Merciful Love. I'd like to focus on two reasons. First, the Image of Divine Mercy speaks directly to the main purpose of the Offering, which is to console or "have mercy" on the Heart of Jesus.

Recall that the Offering is meant to relieve Jesus of the heartache that comes from so much rejection of his love. Well, the way to relieve his heartache is by receiving his mercy. So, in a way, you might say that the Image of Divine Mercy is Jesus' own heart medication. It's like this: Jesus suffers from a terribly painful heart condition, so he's written for himself a prescription for medication that will relieve him of his agony. What's the medication? It's when we receive the rays of his love and mercy and say the prayer, "Jesus, I trust in you" — for this truly consoles his Heart.

Another way that the Divine Mercy Image goes perfectly with the Family Offering is that it serves as a reminder of our invitation to Jesus to come into our homes with his mercy. I mean, without a concrete *reminder*, we might easily forget that we've invited Jesus to come with his mercy and stay in our homes. Also, the image itself becomes a concrete realization of the invitation. It's like this: We invite Jesus to come into our homes, and then, with the Image of Divine Mercy, there he is! And as we've learned from St. Faustina, this image truly is "living" and "grace-filled."[221] Moreover, when you display it in your home in a place of honor where you'll see it daily, it becomes a continual, concrete, physical reminder of the solemn invitation (offering) you and your family have made.

So, I recommend that the Family Offering be accompanied by a Divine Mercy Image Enthronement. By this, I mean that when you make the Offering, you could also solemnly put up an Image of Divine Mercy in a place of honor in your home (if you don't already have an image there). An appropriate prayer for such an enthronement, which could be prayed after making the Offering and in front of the Image of Divine Mercy, is as follows:

> **LEADER:** Jesus, you said to St. Faustina: "I am offering people a vessel with which they are to keep coming for graces to the fountain of mercy. That vessel is this image with the signature: 'Jesus, I trust in You.'[222] By means of this image I shall be granting many graces to souls."[223]
>
> **ALL:** Lord Jesus, through this image of your mercy, please grant us your grace. Whenever we look at it, help us to remember your love and mercy, and fill our hearts with trust. Just as your mercy is depicted in this image as going forth from your pierced Heart, surround our home with the rays of your mercy. May the blood and water that flows forth from your Heart always be upon us! Jesus, we trust in you.

I further recommend concluding such a prayer by praying a Divine Mercy Chaplet. (See endnote 159 for instructions on how to pray it.) Also, it might be a good idea to invite a priest to bless your home and your Image of Divine Mercy. If the priest can't make it, perhaps you can ask him to solemnly bless your image (with others from the parish) on Divine Mercy Sunday. This is appropriate because Jesus asked that the Divine Mercy Image be solemnly blessed on Divine Mercy Sunday and venerated publically.[224]

Endnotes

soug de fausses joies, ce n'était pas mes
rale, car il en fallait un pour me gu
et ce fut Notre Dame des Victoires qu
la neuvaine de messes) Marie sortit dans
onie qui lisait auprès de la fenêtre, en l
mis à appeler presque tout bas: « Maman
à m'entendre toujours appeler ainsi, ne
a longtemps. alors j'appelai plus fort et
antement entrer, mais je ne pouvais dire
ais d'appeler toujours plus fort: « Maman
te [belle] forcée, et inexplicable, et Marie en souffr
nor, après de vains efforts pour me montr
le se mit à genoux auprès de mon lit avec
ant vers la Sainte Vierge et la priant avec
de la vie de son Enfant, Marie obtint ce
rouvant aucun secours sur la terre, la pauv
e vers sa Mère du Ciel, elle la priant de tou
...... tout à coup la Sainte Vierge me
s je n'avais vu rien de si beau, son visag
tendresse ineffable, mais ce qui me pénétra

[1] *Story of a Soul: The Autobiography of St. Thérèse of Lisieux*, trans. John Clarke, OCD, 3rd ed. (Washington, DC: ICS Publications, 1996), p. 174.
[2] See *The Kolbe Reader: The Writings of St. Maximilian Kolbe, OFM Conv.*, ed. and commentary, Fr. Anselm W. Romb, OFM, Cap. (Libertyville, Ill.: Marytown Press, 2007), pp. 61-62.
[3] See *The Second Greatest Story Ever Told: Now Is the Time of Mercy* (Stockbridge: Marian Press, 2015), pp. 56-60. For examples of how Jesus taught St. Faustina about the Offering to Merciful Love "Faustina-style" (which is virtually identical to the Offering Thérèse-style), see pages 73-74 of this book. Also, it's interesting to note that St. Thérèse once appeared to St. Faustina and encouraged her to trust in Jesus (see *Diary of Saint Maria Faustina Kowalska: Divine Mercy in My Soul* [Stockbridge: Marian Press, 1987], 150.
[4] Some of the content from this day's reflection comes from my book *The Second Greatest Story Ever Told*, pp. 17-18.
[5] Emphasis added. (Unless otherwise indicated, as in this case, all emphasis in citations is original.)
[6] English translation of the *Catechism of the Catholic Church: Modifications from the Editio Typica* (Washington, D.C./Vatican: United States Catholic Conference, Inc./Libreria Editrice Vaticana, 1997), 397. Emphasis added.
[7] Ibid., 399.
[8] Ibid.
[9] *Diary*, 731.
[10] *Catechism of the Catholic Church*, 144.
[11] Ibid., 149.
[12] Pope John Paul II, Encyclical Letter *Redemptoris Mater* (*Mother of the Redeemer*), March 25, 1987, 12.
[13] The first blessing is the one we repeat when we pray the Hail Mary: "Blessed are you among women, and blessed is the fruit of your womb!" (Lk 1:42).
[14] *Redemptoris Mater*, 12.
[15] Ibid., 14. Emphasis added.
[16] Ibid., 17.
[17] Ibid.
[18] Ibid.
[19] Ibid.
[20] Ibid.
[21] Second Vatican Council, Dogmatic Constitution on the Church, *Lumen Gentium*, November 21, 1964, 58.
[22] *Redemptoris Mater*, 18.
[23] Ibid., 19.
[24] As we'll learn in Week Three of this retreat and elsewhere, "consoling Jesus" is an important part of St. Thérèse's spirituality.
[25] *Story of a Soul*, p. 188. Saint Faustina writes something similar: "I want to live in the spirit of faith. I accept everything that comes my way as given me by the loving will of God, who sincerely desires my happiness.

And so I will accept with submission and gratitude everything that God sends me" (1549).

[26] That Mary is "the New Eve" is derived from Sacred Scripture, taught by the early Fathers of the Church, and faithfully held throughout the Tradition of the Church. See *Catechism*, 411, 511, 975.

[27] The Fathers of the Church and numerous popes taught that Mary is the "Mediatrix of Grace" and several popes have even used the title "Mediatrix of All Graces." (For instance, Pope John Paul II used the latter title seven times during his pontificate.) Also, see Vatican II's Dogmatic Constitution on the Church, *Lumen Gentium*, 61-62, which describes Mary's role as a Mediatrix.

[28] See *33 Days to Morning Glory: A Do-It-Yourself Retreat In Preparation for Marian Consecration* (Stockbridge: Marian Press, 2011), pp. 97-100.

[29] See *Catechism*, 494.

[30] Because St. Joseph's heroic faith is so essentially linked to that of Mary, his inclusion is implied in the attention here given to the faith of his spouse. See Pope John Paul II, Apostolic Exhortation *Redemptoris Custos*, 4.

[31] Cited by Pope John Paul II in his Apostolic Letter *Divini Amoris Scientia*, October 19, 1997, 10.

[32] Since that time, the popes have added three more saints to the list of the Doctors of the Church, raising the total to 36.

[33] From a testimony given at the beatification process of Zélie Martin and cited in *The Context of Holiness: Psychological and Spiritual Reflections on the Life of St. Thérèse of Lisieux* by Marc Foley, OCD (Washington, D.C.: ICS Publications, 2008), p. 100. On the same page, Foley goes into further detail about Zélie's "excessive fear" and what it was like for her, growing up in a home that "was dominated by 'a certain atmosphere of austerity, constraint and scrupulosity.'"

[34] Full quote: "She becomes emotional very easily. As soon as she does anything wrong, everybody must know it. Yesterday, not meaning to do so, she tore off a small piece of wallpaper. She wanted to tell her Father immediately, and you would have pitied her to see her anxiety. When he returned four hours later and everybody had forgotten about it, she ran at once to Marie, saying: 'Marie, hurry and tell Papa I tore the paper.' Then she awaited her sentence as if she were a criminal … " (*Story of a Soul*, pp. 18-19).

[35] Full quote: "[Thérèse] is very sensitive; when she's said a word too many, or when she's made a mistake, she notices it immediately and, to make up for it, the poor baby has recourse to tears, and she asks for pardons which never end. We tell her she's forgiven but in vain. She goes on crying just the same" (*Letters of St. Thérèse of Lisieux*, trans. John Clarke, OCD, vol. 1, 1877-1890. [Washington, D.C.: ICS Publications, 1982], p. 114).

[36] Ibid.

[37] Conrad De Meester, OCD, *With Empty Hands: The Message of St. Thérèse of Lisieux*, trans. Mary Seymour (Washington, D.C.: ICS Publications, 2002), p. 45.

[38] Cited in ibid., p. 54.
[39] *Letters of St. Thérèse of Lisieux*, vol. 1, p. 226. The titles of the retreat conferences were "Hell, Judgement, Mortal Sin, The Necessity of Making a Good Confession, and Sacrilegious Communion" (*The Context of Holiness*, p. 104).
[40] Cited in *With Empty Hands*, p. 47.
[41] Cited in ibid., p. 42.
[42] *Story of a Soul*, p. 98.
[43] See endnote 126.
[44] *Story of a Soul*, pp. 60-65. See also *The Context of Holiness*, pp. 71-83.
[45] Regarding Thérèse being a victim of bullying, an outcast, and loner who couldn't join in the games of the others or comb her own hair, see *Story of a Soul*, pp. 53-54, 75, 81-83, 87. See also *The Context of Holiness*, pp. 37-42.
[46] *Story of a Soul*, p. 83.
[47] Ibid., pp. 83-4.
[48] Ibid., p. 27.
[49] Ibid.
[50] See *With Empty Hands*, pp. 38-39.
[51] *Story of a Soul*, p. 198.
[52] Ibid., p. 105.
[53] Ibid., p. 207. Emphasis added.
[54] Ibid., pp. 207-8.
[55] Conrad De Meester, OCD, *The Power of Confidence: Genesis and Structure of the "Way of Spiritual Childhood" of St. Thérèse of Lisieux*, trans. Susan Conroy (New York: Alba House, 1998), p. 12.
[56] *Catechism*, 1846. Emphasis added. Also, in a *Regina Caeli* message for Divine Mercy Sunday, 2008, Pope Benedict XVI stated, "Indeed, mercy is the central nucleus of the Gospel message; it is the very name of God, the Face with which he revealed himself in the Old Covenant and fully in Jesus Christ, the incarnation of creative and redemptive Love."
[57] *Story of a Soul*, p. 208. Emphasis added.
[58] Pope Pius XII stated that St. Thérèse "rediscovers the Gospel" on the occasion of the consecration of the Basilica of Lisieux on July 11, 1954 (*AAS* 46 [1954], pp. 404-8).
[59] *Story of a Soul*, pp. 258-59.
[60] Cited in *With Empty Hands*, p. 104.
[61] *Diary*, 723.
[62] Cited in *With Empty Hands*, pp. 112-13.
[63] Ibid., p. 113.
[64] Cited in *The Power of Confidence*, p. 283. Of course, this does not mean that little souls can never be successful in the practice of virtue, but when they are, Thérèse describes what their attitude should be:

> To be little is also to not attribute to oneself the virtues that one practices, believing oneself capable of anything, but to recognize that God places this treasure of virtue in the hands

of His little child, to be used when necessary; but it remains always God's treasure (ibid., p. 228).

Also, in his book *The Name of God Is Mercy: A Conversation with Andrea Tornielli*, trans. Oonagh Stransky, (New York: Random House, 2016), Pope Francis explains why God might allow someone to fall into sin:

> At times I have surprised myself by thinking that a few very rigid people would do well to slip a little, so that they could remember that they are sinners and thus meet Jesus. I think back to the words of God's servant John Paul I, who during a Wednesday audience said, "The Lord loves humility so much that sometimes he permits serious sins. Why? In order that those who committed these sins may, after repenting, remain humble (p. 70).

[65] St. Thérèse knew that God does not judge based on appearances. Rather, he judges the heart. So, what may seem to us like a hopeless case — for instance, a person stuck in the cycle of addiction or someone with an insufferable temperament — may in fact be a hidden saint, particularly loved by God because of their humility and unseen efforts. Conrad de Meester explains Thérèse's teaching on this point:

> Thérèse knew how God's life could lie hidden below the surface of a human psyche and temperament, and that some souls were much closer to God than might be apparent if they were judged merely by their struggles and inhibitions. "What we think of as negligence," Thérèse wrote, "is very often heroism in the eyes of God." She warned Céline: "On the last day, you will be astonished to see your sisters freed from all their imperfections, and they will appear as great saints." Although such "little souls" might pass unnoticed and have nothing to boast about, they are great in the eyes of God, for in their poverty they are full of hope (*With Empty Hands*, p. 110).

One sister that Thérèse probably had in mind as one with a lot of "imperfections" was Sr. Marie of St. Joseph, who suffered from mental illness and lived on the periphery of the Lisieux community, because nobody was willing to work with her, except for Thérèse. Thérèse got to know Sr. Marie's tormented soul more than anyone and once shared with her sister Pauline (Mother Agnes):

> If you knew her as well as I do, you would see that she is not responsible for all of the things that seem so awful to us. ... [S]he is to be pitied ... she is like an old clock that has to be re-wound every quarter of an hour. Yes, it is as bad as that. ... [I]f I had an infirmity such as hers, and so defective a

> spirit, I would not do any better than she does, and then I would despair (cited in *The Context of Holiness*, p. 44).

But Sr. Marie of St. Joseph did not despair. Even after the death of her one true friend in the convent (Thérèse), even after her mental illness caused her to have to leave the convent at the age of 55 after 28 years of religious life, even after "years of wondering aimlessly about the French countryside" (ibid., p. 51) — amazingly — she could still write the following words to Mother Agnes, words that reveal her hidden sanctity:

> The work of sanctification which my beloved Thérèse began so lovingly in me before she died continues. And I can say in all sincerity that — my house is at rest. And I live now in complete abandonment. As long as I love Jesus, and He and Thérèse are pleased, nothing else matters to me (Cited in ibid., p. 51).

[66] Pope Francis, homily at the parish of St. Anna in the Vatican, Fifth Sunday of Lent, March 17, 2013.
[67] Cited in *The Power of Confidence*, p. 221.
[68] Cited in ibid., p. 222.
[69] Cited in ibid., p. 93.
[70] Paraphrasing and applying Mary's Magnificat to herself in order to express her gratitude to God for having made her so vividly aware of her littleness, Thérèse writes:

> The Almighty has done great things in the soul of His divine Mother's child, and the greatest thing is to have shown her her littleness, her impotence (*Story of a Soul*, p. 210).

[71] *Story of a Soul*, p. 256.
[72] Regarding trust being the key to receiving God's mercy, Jesus told St. Faustina:

> The graces of My mercy are drawn by means of one vessel only, and that is — trust. The more a soul trusts, the more it will receive. Souls that trust boundlessly are a great comfort to Me, because I pour all the treasures of My graces into them. I rejoice that they ask for much, because it is My desire to give much, very much. On the other hand, I am sad when souls ask for little, when they narrow their hearts (*Diary*, 1578).

[73] Thérèse believed she would become a great saint, but her faith and hope in this regard was not based on pride but, rather, humility, as is clear from the following passage:

> I considered that I was born for *glory* and when I searched out

> the means of attaining it, God inspired in me the sentiments I have just described. He made me understand my own glory would not be evident to the eyes of mortals, that it would consist in becoming a great *saint!* This desire could certainly appear daring if one were to consider how weak and imperfect I was, and how, after seven years in the religious life, I still am weak and imperfect. I always feel, however, the same bold confidence of becoming a great saint because I don't count on my merits since I have *none*, but I trust in Him who is Virtue and Holiness. God alone, content with my weak efforts, will raise me to Himself and make me a *saint*, clothing me in His infinite merits (*Story of a Soul*, p. 72).

[74] *Story of a Soul*, p. 200.

[75] Pope Francis, address to the priests of the Diocese of Rome, March 6, 2014. (Translation by ZENIT.) A related quote from Pope Francis came during an interview on the plane ride back from World Youth Day in Brazil on July 28, 2013:

> I believe that this is the season of mercy. This new era we have entered, and the many problems in the Church — like the poor witness given by some priests, problems of corruption in the Church, the problem of clericalism for example — have left so many people hurt, left so much hurt. The Church is a mother: she has to go out to heal those who are hurting, with mercy. If the Lord never tires of forgiving, we have no other choice than this: first of all, to care for those who are hurting. The Church is a mother, and she must travel this path of mercy and find a form of mercy for all. When the prodigal son returned home, I don't think his father told him: "You, sit down and listen: what did you do with the money?" No! He celebrated! Then, perhaps, when the son was ready to speak, he spoke. The Church has to do this, when there is someone… not only wait for them, but go out and find them! That is what mercy is. And I believe that this is a *kairos*: this time is a *kairos* of mercy. But John Paul II had the first intuition of this, when he began with Faustina Kowalska, the Divine Mercy… He had something, he had intuited that this was a need in our time (Vatican translation).

Later, in his book *The Name of God is Mercy*, the Pope further elaborates on these comments on the plane:

> Yes, I believe that this is a time for mercy. The Church is showing her maternal side, her motherly face, to a humanity that is wounded. She does not wait for the wounded to knock on her doors, she looks for them on the streets, she

> gathers them in, she embraces them, she takes care of them, she makes them feel loved. And so, as I said, and I am ever more convinced of it, this is a *kairos*, our era is a *kairos* of mercy, an opportune time (p. 6).

By the way, Pope Francis has a great devotion to St. Thérèse and often receives a white rose from she who said, "[A]fter my death [I] will send down a shower of roses" (Cited in *The Passion of Thérèse of Lisieux* by Guy Gaucher [New York: Crossroad, 1989], p. 194). To learn more about the Pope's devotion and his white roses, see *The Great Reformer: Francis and the Making of a Radical Pope* by Austen Ivereigh (New York: Henry Holt and Company, 2014), pp. 338-340.

[76] Niels Christian Hvidt, *Christian Prophecy: The Post-Biblical Tradition* (Oxford/New York: Oxford University Press, 2007), p. vii. Emphasis added.

[77] Saint Louis de Montfort also taught that God would raise up in our time, from among the weak and broken, great saints, "who shall surpass most of the other saints." See *33 Days to Morning Glory*, pp. 21-23.

[78] *Diary*, 47.

[79] In the following prayer, we learn that St. Faustina had hope of becoming one of the greatest of saints, even though she was very weak and broken, because she trusted completely in the power of God's mercy:

> O God, one in the Holy Trinity, I want to love You as no human soul has ever loved You before; and although I am utterly miserable and small, I have, nevertheless, cast the anchor of my trust deep down into the abyss of Your mercy ... . In spite of my great misery I fear nothing, but hope to sing You a hymn of glory forever. Let no soul, even the most miserable fall prey to doubt; for, as long as one is alive, each one can become a great saint, so great is the power of God's grace. It remains only for us not to oppose God's action (*Diary*, 283).

Later, Jesus himself revealed to St. Faustina the importance of trust for receiving the graces of his mercy, which form us into saints:

> Let souls who are striving for perfection particularly adore My mercy, because the abundance of graces which I grant them flows from My mercy. I desire that these souls distinguish themselves by boundless trust in My mercy. I myself will attend to the sanctification of such souls. I will provide them with everything they need to attain sanctity. The graces of My mercy are drawn by means of one vessel only, and that is — trust. The more a soul trusts, the more it will receive. Souls that trust boundlessly are a great comfort to Me, because I pour all the treasures of My graces into them. I rejoice that they ask for much, because it is My desire to give much, very

> much. On the other hand, I am sad when souls ask for little, when they narrow their hearts (1577-1578).

[80] *Story of a Soul*, p. 174.
[81] "Letter 197 to Sr. Marie of the Sacred Heart, September 17, 1896," *Letters of St. Thérèse of Lisieux*, trans. John Clarke, OCD, vol. 2, 1890-1897. (Washington, DC: ICS Publications, 1982), pp. 998-1000.
[82] *St. Thérèse of Lisieux: By Those Who Knew Her* ed. and trans. Christopher O'Mahony. (Dublin: Veritas Publications, 1995), p. 49.
[83] Ibid.
[84] *With Empty Hands*, p. 71.
[85] Cited in *The Power of Confidence*, p. 167.
[86] Cited in ibid. Emphasis added.
[87] Cited in ibid.
[88] Cited in ibid.
[89] *Story of a Soul*, p. 180. Emphasis added.
[90] Ibid.
[91] Ibid., pp. 180-1.
[92] Marie-Eugene of the Child Jesus, OCD, *I Want to See God: A Practical Synthesis of Carmelite Spirituality*, trans. M. Verda Clare, CSC (Chicago: Fides Publishers Association, 1953), p. 25. Emphasis added.
[93] To further help us understand how "Jesus actually 'needs' us and that we can give relief to his Sacred and Merciful Heart," see the first section of Appendix One, "How We Can Console Jesus."
[94] *Diary*, 367. Emphasis added.
[95] Ibid., 1074.
[96] Ibid., 1705.
[97] This is perhaps why God would accept the prayer of people who offered themselves as victim souls to divine Justice — it's because Jesus did it first! Also, the fact that, on the Cross, Jesus is a victim to divine Justice certainly does not exclude him from being a spiritual victim in other ways.
[98] See *33 Days to Morning Glory*, pp. 70-72.
[99] Cited by Geneviève of the Holy Face (Céline Martin) in *My Sister St. Thérèse*, trans. Carmelite Sisters of New York of Conseils et Souvenirs (Rockford, Ill.: TAN Books and Publishers, 1997), p. 80. Elsewhere she writes:

> The soul which offers itself to love does not ask for suffering, but, in delivering itself up entirely to the designs of love, it accepts all that Providence permits for it of joys, labor, trials, and it counts on infinite mercy for everything (Cited in Pére Jean du Coeur de Jésus d'Elbée, *I Believe in Love: Retreat Conferences on the Interior Life*, trans. Marilyn Teichert and Madeleine Stebbins [Petersham, MA: St. Bede's Publications, 1974], p. 144).

Given these two statements of Sr. Geneviève (above and in the body text), I dare say that she may have a deeper and more nuanced grasp of the nature of the suffering that comes with the Offering to Merciful Love than does her sister Pauline (Mother Agnes of Jesus), who simply testified that, according to Thérèse, "to give yourself to love was to give yourself up to suffering" (*By Those Who Knew Her*, p. 47). But what was the nature of this suffering? As far as I can tell, it is only Sr. Geneviève who expands on this (in the aforementioned citations), which puts little souls at ease. Indeed, the Offering to Merciful Love is not to offer oneself to divine Justice and its harsh punishments. In fact, Sr. Geneviève explicitly states that it "does not ask for suffering." Rather, it's a request to receive what Thérèse calls "infinite tenderness," and as Geneviève put it, "it accepts all that Providence permits for it" not only of "labor and trials" but also of "joys," and "it counts on infinite mercy for everything."

[100] Here's part of the Church's teaching on purgatory from the *Catechism*:

> All who die in God's grace and friendship, but still imperfectly purified, are indeed assured of their eternal salvation; but after death they undergo purification, so as to achieve the holiness necessary to enter the joy of heaven.
>
> The Church gives the name Purgatory to this final purification of the elect, which is entirely different from the punishment of the damned. ... The tradition of the Church, by reference to certain texts of Scripture speaks of a cleansing fire (1030-1031).

[101] *Diary*, 20. Emphasis added.

[102] *Story of a Soul*, p. 181.

[103] Cited in *The Power of Confidence*, p. 344.

[104] Cited in ibid., p. 347.

[105] Yes, Thérèse actually used the word "easy" to describe her Little Way:

> My way is all love and trust. ... [P]erfection seems easy to me. I see that it is enough to realize one's nothingness, and to give oneself wholly, like a child, into the arms of God (cited in Gaucher, p. 167).

Saint Faustina even went so far as to describe holiness according to the path of mercy as "very easy":

> O my Jesus, how very easy it is to become holy; all that is needed is a bit of good will. If Jesus sees this little bit of good will in the soul, He hurries to give Himself to the soul, and nothing can stop Him, neither shortcomings or falls — absolutely nothing. Jesus is anxious to help that soul, and if it is faithful to this grace from God, it can very soon attain the highest holiness possible for a creature here on earth. God is very generous and does not deny His grace to anyone. Indeed He gives more than what we ask of Him (*Diary*, 291)

[106] Cited in *The Power of Confidence*, p. 348.
[107] Cited in ibid., p. 347.
[108] Cited in "The Teaching of St. Thérèse of Lisieux on Purgatory" by Hubert van Dijk, ORC, trans. "Pére de la Trinité," OCD, at www.franscican-sfo.org/ap/litfwrpu.htm (accessed January 10, 2012). Webmaster's note: This article, in German, appears in the December 2001 and the January 2002 issue of *Der Fels* at www.der-fels.de/2001/12-2001.pdf and www.der-fels.de/2002/01-2002.pdf. See also *The Power of Confidence*, pp. 347-348.

Now, regarding the teaching that "unshakable trust ... purifies you" and ensures "that you will not have to go to purgatory," Thérèse is in good company. For instance, in the book *Trustful Surrender to Divine Providence: The Secret to Peace and Happiness* by Fr. Jean Baptiste Saint-Jure and St. Claude de la Colombière and translated by Paul Garvin (Rockford, Ill.: TAN Books and Publishers, 1984), we read the following, which also ties in with Thérèse's idea that we'll learn on Day 21, namely, that the Offering to Merciful Love causes one to become a "martyr of love":

> [I]t is the teaching of great masters of the spiritual life that a person who, at the point of death, makes an act of perfect conformity to the will of God [i.e., an expression of "unshakable trust"] will be delivered not only from Hell but also from Purgatory, even if he has committed all the sins in the world. "The reason," says St. Alphonsus, "is that he who accepts death with perfect resignation acquires similar merit to that of a martyr who has voluntarily given his life for Christ, and even amid the greatest sufferings he will die happily and joyfully" (pp. 61-62).

[109] Cited in van Dijk.
[110] Cited in ibid. (See also *The Power of Confidence*, p. 348.)
[111] Cited in ibid. (See also ibid.)
[112] I've written a whole book explaining how we can show mercy and so hope to receive it. It's called *'You Did It to Me': A Practical Guide to Mercy in Action* (Stockbridge: Marian Press, 2014).
[113] Cited in *The Power of Confidence*, p. 347.
[114] Saint Thérèse seems to have made a similar prayer: "Yes, my God, everything that you will, but have pity on me!" (*Story of a Soul*, p. 270).
[115] *Story of a Soul*, p. 195.
[116] Regarding rejected mercy being "free for the taking," consider the following words of Jesus to St. Faustina recorded in her *Diary*:

> I desire to bestow My graces upon souls but they do not want to accept them. You, at least, come to Me as often as possible and take these graces they do not want to accept. In this way you will console My Heart (367).

> My daughter, take the graces that others spurn; take as many as you can carry (454).
>
> I want to give myself to souls and to fill them with My love, but few there are who want to accept all the graces My love has intended for them. My grace is not lost; if the soul for whom it was intended does not accept it, another soul takes it (1017).

[117] Ibid., p. 180.
[118] Ibid., pp. 276-277. Numbers to each paragraph added.
[119] Seeing the merits of others as also one's own seems to be the secret to overcoming feelings of envy regarding the spiritual goods of others. For example, when Thérèse's sister Céline said to the future saint, "What I envy about you are your good works," Thérèse responded by quoting Johannes Tauler:

> "If I love the good that is in my neighbour as much as he loves it himself, that good is as much mine as it is his." Through this communion I can enrich myself with all the good that there is in heaven and on earth, in the angels, in the saints and in all those who love God (cited in the Study Edition of *Story of a Soul*, prepared by Marc Foley, OCD [Washington, D.C.: ICS Publications, 2005], p. 107).

[120] People sometimes allow the devil to take possession of their souls. They become "possessed." Here, St. Thérèse is asking to become possessed *by God.*
[121] In answer to the question of whether Thérèse's words about Holy Communion remaining in her were to be taken literally or metaphorically, Thérèse's sister Pauline (Mother Agnes) replied:

> She often enlarged on these ideas when speaking to me, and I am certain she meant them literally. Her loving confidence in our Lord made her extraordinarily daring in the things she asked him for. When she thought of his all-powerful love, she had no doubts about anything (*By Those Who Knew Her*, p. 46).

Like the Saint of the Little Way, St. Faustina also received the grace of having Holy Communion remain within her:

> September 29, [1937]. Today, I have come to understand many of God's mysteries. I have come to know that Holy Communion remains in me until the next Holy Communion. A vivid and clearly felt presence of God continues in my soul. The awareness of this plunges me into deep recollection, without the slightest effort on my part. My heart is a living

> tabernacle in which the living Host is reserved. I have never sought God in some far-off place, but within myself. It is in the depths of my own being that I commune with my God (*Diary*, 1302).

[122] To learn how we can "console" Jesus, see the first section of Appendix One, "How We Can Console Jesus." Also, on this topic, it's interesting to note that St. Thérèse took the religious name "Sr. Thérèse of the Child Jesus and of the Holy Face." The "Child Jesus" part should be clear in light of the saint's emphasis on the importance of having a childlike trust in God. But why did she pick "the Holy Face"? I believe it has to do with her "practice of familiarity with Jesus" (see endnote 141) and her emphasis on having a deep, personal relationship with Jesus that's based on reciprocity and mutual love. For, indeed, the face is the window to the soul and, in a certain sense, most reveals the person. Moreover, the Holy Face of Jesus has a special note, namely, his sorrow and suffering. That is, the Holy Face is not a smiling, happy face. It's the face of Christ in his Passion. But this provides perhaps the most important motivation for Thérèse's familiarity with Jesus, because his broken, beaten, sorrowful face invites her to "console" him. At the same time, it consoles her. She herself explains all this in the following lines of a poem she wrote about the Holy Face called, "My Heaven on Earth":

> Ah! you know, your sweet Face
> Is for me Heaven on earth.
> My love discovers the charms
> Of your Face adorned with tears.
> I smile through my own tears
> When I contemplate your sorrows…
>
> Oh! To console you I want
> To live unknown on earth!…
>
> Your Face is my only Homeland…
> It's the Lily of the Valley
> Whose mysterious perfume
> Consoles my exiled soul,
> Making it taste the peace of Heaven.
> (*The Poetry of Saint Thérèse of Lisieux*, trans. Donald Kinney, OCD [Washington, D.C.: ICS Publications, 1996], p. 109.)

[123] Cited in *The Power of Confidence*, p. 302.
[124] *Story of a Soul*, p. 181.
[125] Cited by Patrick Ahern, in *Maurice and Thérèse: The Story of a Love* (New York: Doubleday, 1998), p. 139.
[126] Thérèse understood well the power of God's grace to cleanse her "in one instant." For example, as we learned on Day 8, when she was 14 years old, she experienced the grace of her "Christmas conversion," which im-

mediately gave her the strength to overcome the deep, emotional sensitivity that had dogged her since her early childhood. Describing this grace, she writes:

> The work I had been unable to do in ten years was done by Jesus in one instant, contenting himself with my good will which was never lacking. I could say to Him like His apostles: "Master, I fished all night and caught nothing." More merciful to me than He was to His disciples, Jesus took the net Himself, cast it, and drew it in filled with fish (*Story of a Soul*, pp. 98-99).

[127] That's not quite how the famous Carmelite and Doctor of the Church, St. John of the Cross, put it, but you get the idea. Basically, the longing of the soul for God becomes so intense that the thread of this life is broken. In a letter to her sister Pauline (Mother Agnes), St. Thérèse writes about this kind of death, beginning with a quote from St. John of the Cross:

> "Tear through the veil of this sweet encounter!" I've always applied these words to the death of love that I desire. Love will not wear out the veil of my life. It will tear it suddenly (cited in Gaucher, p. 222).

And, again, the death of love allows one to bypass purgatory as Thérèse implicitly says in the text of the Offering when she describes the flight of her soul to God as being "without any delay." Saint Faustina makes this point a bit more explicit in the following passage from her *Diary*:

> God's mercy sometimes touches the sinner at the last moment in a wondrous and mysterious way. Outwardly, it seems as if everything were lost, but it is not so. The soul, illumined by a ray of God's powerful final grace, turns to God in the last moment with such a power of love that, in an instant, it receives from God forgiveness of sin and punishment, while outwardly it shows no sign either of repentance or of contrition, because souls [at that stage] no longer react to external things. Oh, how beyond comprehension is God's mercy! (1698).

Notice here that God gives such souls "forgiveness of sin *and punishment*." That means no purgatory! And Faustina even refers to the soul that receives this grace as "the sinner." Certainly God can give this "final grace" even to someone who turns to Him from a state of mortal sin — how great is the power of God's mercy! Also, how great is the power of *intercessory prayer*. I say that because our prayers truly can obtain for others this amazing mercy, even for those who seem hopelessly lost. I also say that because St. Faustina herself prefaces the above citation by saying, "I often attend upon the dying and through entreaties obtain for them trust in God's mercy, and I implore God for an abundance of divine grace, which is always victorious."

[128] Saint John of the Cross, *The Living Flame of Love*, commentary on stanza 1, line 6 (cited in Gaucher, p. 221).

[129] *Story of a Soul*, pp. 276-77.

[130] Ibid., p. 181.

[131] See *The Power of Confidence*, p. 157.

[132] *Story of a Soul*, p. 181.

[133] Ibid., p. 149.

[134] Regarding mortal sin and venial sin, the *Catechism* teaches:

> Sins are rightly evaluated according to their gravity. The distinction between mortal and venial sin, already evident in Scripture, became part of the tradition of the Church. It is corroborated by human experience.
>
> *Mortal sin* destroys charity in the heart of man by a grave violation of God's law; it turns man away from God, who is his ultimate end and his beatitude, by preferring an inferior good to him. Venial sin allows charity to subsist, even though it offends and wounds it (1854-1855).

Also, according the spiritual theologian, Jordan Aumann, OP, "it is necessary to distinguish between venial sins committed out of weakness, surprise, or lack of advertence and deliberation, and those that are committed coldly and with complete awareness that one thereby displeases God" (Spiritual Theology [Huntington, Ind.: Our Sunday Visitor, 1980], p. 153). The latter kind of sin is what I mean by "deliberate venial sin," the kind of sin that is chosen after some reflection and with awareness that it is displeasing to God.

[135] *Story of a Soul*, pp. 83-84.

[136] Ibid., p. 224.

[137] See *The Power of Confidence*, p. 241, and Gaucher, p. 172.

[138] *Story of a Soul*, p. 259.

[139] Ibid.

[140] Cited in Gaucher, p. 186.

[141] St. Thérèse often described her Little Way as a path that excludes fear, which makes sense because "There is no fear in love, but perfect love casts out fear" (1 Jn 4:18). For instance, she wrote: "I am far from being on the way of fear" (*Story of a Soul*, p. 173). "My nature was such that fear made me recoil; with *love* not only did I advance, I actually *flew*" (Ibid., p. 174). "Ah, the Lord is so good to me it is quite impossible for me to fear him" (Ibid., p. 250). We also read the following commentary and quote compilation from Guy Gaucher:

> Anticipating the liturgical reform by some sixty years, Thérèse used the familiar [not formal] form of "Tu" ... when

> speaking of Jesus. She kissed "the face" and "both cheeks," and not the feet of the crucifix as was the custom at that time. Looking at a picture of two children with Jesus, she said: "The other little one does not please me as much; he's acting like an adult. He's been told something, and he knows he must respect Jesus." In heaven she would not be like the Seraphim who "cover themselves with their wings before God." (Gaucher, pp. 149-150).

Thérèse does, however, recognize that the "practice of familiarity with Jesus" isn't easy, acknowledging that "we don't get to this in a single day" (cited in Ahern, p. 167). So, she tries to explain "by a very simple example, how much Jesus loves even very imperfect souls, who trust in Him":

> I'm thinking of a father who has two children who are mischievous and disobedient, and when he comes to punish them he sees one who trembles and draws away from him in fright, knowing in the bottom of his heart that he deserves to be punished. His brother, on the contrary, throws himself into his father's arms, protesting that he is sorry for hurting him, that he loves him, and that to prove it he will be good from now on. Then if this child asks his father to *punish* him with a *kiss*, I doubt that the heart of the happy father will be able to resist the childlike confidence of his son, of whose sincerity he is sure. He's well aware that the child will often fall back into the these same faults, but he's always ready to forgive him, provided the boy always grasps him by the heart. I say nothing about the first child .... Surely [we] know ... whether his father can love him as much as the other and treat him with the same indulgence (cited in ibid., pp. 167-168).

But what does wound Jesus, Thérèse explains, is "only when his friends, ignoring their continual indelicacies, make a habit out of them and don't ask forgiveness for them" (cited in ibid., p. 189). Pope Francis calls this sinful situation "corruption":

> Corruption is the sin which, rather than being recognised as such and rendering us humble, is elevated to a system; it becomes a mental habit, a way of living. We no longer feel the need for forgiveness and mercy, but we justify ourselves and our behaviours. ... The repentant sinner, who sins again and again because of his weakness, will find forgiveness if he acknowledges his need for mercy. The corrupt man is the one who sins but does not repent, who sins and pretends to be Christian, and it is this double life that is scandalous. ... Sin, especially if repeated, can lead to corruption, not quantitatively — in the sense that a certain number of sins makes a person corrupt — but rather

> qualitatively: habits are formed that limit one's capacity for love and create a false sense of self-sufficiency. ... The corrupt man tires of asking for forgiveness and ends up believing that he doesn't need to ask for it any more. We don't become corrupt people overnight. It is a long, slippery slope that cannot be identified simply as a series of sins. One may be a great sinner and never fall into corruption if hearts feel their own weakness. That small opening allows the strength of God to enter (*The Name of God is Mercy*, pp. 81-82.)

So, we need "only" fear becoming corrupt. We need only fear the sin of presumption where we seek to "justify ourselves and our behaviors" without asking for forgiveness and mercy. We need only fear becoming "one who sins but does not repent," one who "tires of asking for forgiveness and ends up believing that he doesn't need to ask for it any more." Apart from falling into the evil habit of corruption, Thérèse would say that there is no reason to be afraid.

Now, lest we think that Thérèse is alone in boldly speaking about not fearing God and being so familiar with him, we read the following from St. Faustina: "Even if I were to hear the most terrifying things about God's justice, I would not fear Him at all, because I have come to know Him well" (*Diary*, 589). And also:

> [E]ven if I were to be told of God's justice and of how even the pure spirits tremble and cover their faces before Him, saying endlessly, "Holy," which would seem to suggest that my familiarity with God would be to the detriment of His honor and majesty, [I would reply,] "O no, no, and once again, no!" (ibid, 947).

[142] Cited in *Story of a Soul*, p. 259. Although the reality of God's mercy for sinners "is beyond the power of words to express," St. Faustina does try to lift the veil of the mystery in the following passages from her *Diary*:

> I often communicate with persons who are dying and obtain the divine mercy for them. Oh, how great is the goodness of God, greater than we can understand. There are moments and there are mysteries of the divine mercy over which the heavens are astounded. Let our judgment of souls cease, for God's mercy upon them is extraordinary (1684).

> I often attend upon the dying and through entreaties obtain for them trust in God's mercy, and I implore God for an abundance of divine grace, which is always victorious. God's mercy sometimes touches the sinner at the last moment in a wondrous and mysterious way. Outwardly, it seems as if everything were lost, but it is not so. The soul, illumined by a ray of God's pow-

> erful final grace, turns to God in the last moment with such a power of love that, in an instant, it receives from God forgiveness of sin and punishment, while outwardly it shows no sign either of repentance or of contrition, because souls [at that stage] no longer react to external things. Oh, how beyond comprehension is God's mercy! (1698).

Also, regarding the idea of God's amazing mercy for sinners being "beyond the power of words to express," Jesus once said to St. Faustina, "My daughter, do you think you have written enough about My mercy? What you have written is but a drop compared to the ocean. I am Love and Mercy itself" (1273).

[143] Cited in Ahern, p. 190. Emphasis added.

[144] The whole citation is as follows:

> You see what you are of yourself, but do not be frightened at this. If I were to reveal to you the whole misery that you are, you would die of terror. However, be aware of what you are. Because you are such great misery, I have revealed to you the whole ocean of My mercy. I seek and desire souls like you, but they are few. Your great trust in Me forces Me to continuously grant you graces. You have great and incomprehensible rights over My Heart, for you are a daughter of complete trust (*Diary*, 718).

On this same topic, St. Faustina wrote the following about herself: "There is no soul more wretched than I am, as I truly know myself, and I am astounded that divine Majesty stoops so low" (440).

[145] Gaucher, p. 147.

[146] See *Story of a Soul*, p. 158: "[T]he more one advances, the more one sees the goal is still far off. And now I am simply resigned to see myself always imperfect and in this I find my joy."

[147] Ibid., p. 256. Emphasis added.

[148] *Story of a Soul*, pp. 276-277.

[149] Cited in *The Power of Confidence*, pp. 248-9.

[150] The spirituality of offering ourselves along with Christ during the "Through him, and with him, and in him … " supercharged moment of the Mass also provides us with an opportunity to simplify our prayer for others. In fact, I believe that it is in the context of the offering of the Mass that we can best understand the following words of St. Thérèse (especially "draw me, we shall run") that reveal how she found a simple way of interceding for others:

> Since I have two brothers and my little Sisters, the novices, if I wanted to ask for each soul what each one needed and go into detail about it, the days would not be long enough and I fear I would forget something important. For simple souls

> there must be no complicated ways; as I am of their number, one morning during my thanksgiving, Jesus gave me a simple means of accomplishing my mission.
>
> He made me understand these words of the Canticle of Canticles: "*DRAW ME, WE SHALL RUN after you in the odor of your ointments*" (1:3). O Jesus, it is not even necessary to say: "*When drawing me, draw the souls whom I love!*" This simple statement: "Draw me" suffices; I understand, Lord, that when a soul allows herself to be captivated by the *odor of your ointments*, she cannot run alone, all the souls whom she loves follow in her train; this is done without constraint, without effort, it is a natural consequence of her attraction for You. Just as a torrent, throwing itself with impetuosity into the ocean, drags after it everything it encounters in its passage, in the same way, O Jesus, the soul who plunges into the shoreless ocean of Your Love, draws with her all the treasures she possesses. Lord, You know it, I have no other treasures than the souls it has pleased You to unite to mine; it is You who entrusted these treasures to me (*Story of a Soul*, p. 254).

For more information on the spirituality of offering ourselves with Christ to the Father at the Mass, see my book *The 'One Thing' Is Three: How the Most Holy Trinity Explains Everything* (Stockbridge: Marian Press, 2012), pp. 255-283.

[151] The French philosopher Blaise Pascal said that "the sole cause of man's unhappiness is that he does not know how to stay quietly in his own room" (*Pensées*. trans. A.J. Krailsheimer [London: Penguin Classics, 1966], 136). He also stated: "Man finds nothing so intolerable as to be in a state of complete rest ... without occupation, without diversion ... " (622).

[152] For a powerful example of this sentiment, watch the YouTube video of Johnny Cash's rendition of "Hurt" by Nine Inch Nails.

[153] Thérèse believed she could only do "little things" for God. For instance, she wrote:

> I made a resolution to give myself up more than ever to a serious and mortified life. When I say mortified, this is not to give the impression that I performed acts of penance. Alas, *I never made any*. Far from resembling beautiful souls who practiced every kind of mortification from their childhood, I had no attraction for this. Undoubtedly this stemmed from my cowardliness, for I could have, like Céline, found a thousand ways of making myself suffer. Instead of this I allowed myself to be wrapped in cotton wool and fattened up like a little bird that needs no penance. My mortifications consisted in breaking my will, always so ready to impose itself on others, in holding back a reply, in rendering little services without any

> recognition, in not leaning my back against a support when seated, etc., etc. It was through the practice of these nothings … (*Story of a Soul*, pp. 143-144).
>
> [I prove my love for God] by all the smallest things and doing them through love (Ibid., p. 196).
>
> [Y]ou can see that I am a very little soul and that I can offer God only very little things (Ibid., p. 250).

[154] Cited in Ahern, p. 52.

[155] Actually, according to the testimony of St. Faustina, in this time of great mercy, the Lord wants to make us saints not just to save the world but also *to prepare it for his final coming*. For instance, she records the following in her *Diary*:

> When I became aware of God's great plans for me, I was frightened at their greatness and felt myself quite incapable of fulfilling them, and I began to avoid interior conversations with Him, filling up the time with vocal prayer. I did this out of humility, but I soon recognized it was not true humility, but rather a great temptation from the devil. When, on one occasion, instead of interior prayer, I took up a book of spiritual reading, I heard these words spoken distinctly and forcefully within my soul, *You will prepare the world for My final coming*. These words moved me deeply, and although I pretended not to hear them, I understood them very well and had no doubt about them (429).

There are several other passages like this from the *Diary* of St. Faustina (see 635, 848, 965, 1160, 1588, 1146). Of course, such passages do not mean we know the day or the hour of the Lord's coming, but they do give a greater sense of urgency to the present time of mercy. To learn more, see Appendix One of *The Second Greatest Story Ever Told*, "Regarding the Lord's Final Coming."

It is interesting to note here that Pope John Paul II explicitly brought together this topic of preparing the world for the Lord's final coming with a consecration or "entrustment" to Divine Mercy. I say that because, during his homily for the dedication of the Shrine of Divine Mercy in Krakow-Łagiewniki, Poland, on August 17, 2002, the Pope entrusted the whole world to Divine Mercy and included a passage from the *Diary* of St. Faustina that speaks of the Lord's final coming:

> Today, therefore, in this Shrine, I wish solemnly to entrust the world to Divine Mercy. I do so with the burning desire that the message of God's merciful love, proclaimed here through Saint Faustina, may be made known to all the peo-

> ples of the earth and fill their hearts with hope. May this message radiate from this place to our beloved homeland and throughout the world. May the binding promise of the Lord Jesus be fulfilled: from here there must go forth "the spark which will prepare the world for his final coming" (see *Diary*, 1732). This spark needs to be lighted by the grace of God. This fire of mercy needs to be passed on to the world. In the mercy of God the world will find peace and mankind will find happiness!

[156] Georgina Molyneux, *Cure D'Ars: A Memoir of Jean-Baptiste-Marie Vianney* (London: Richard Bentley, New Burlington Street, 1869), p. 157.
[157] See endnote 3.
[158] In his encyclical letter on Divine Mercy, *Dives in Misericordia*, Pope John Paul II spoke about the importance of making a plea to God for mercy in our time. In fact, the entire last chapter of the encyclical is a sustained teaching on the importance of *calling out for God's mercy even "with loud cries"* (15). The Pope says that "[t]hese 'loud cries' [for mercy] should be the mark of the Church of our times" (15).
[159] The following passage from the *Diary* of St. Faustina provides the origin of the Chaplet of Divine Mercy and reveals its power:

> In the evening, when I was in my [room], I saw an Angel, the executor of divine wrath. He was clothed in a dazzling robe, his face gloriously bright, a cloud beneath his feet. From the cloud, bolts of thunder and flashes of lightning were springing into his hands; and from his hand they were going forth, and only then were they striking the earth. When I saw this sign of divine wrath which was about to strike the earth, and in particular a certain place, which for good reasons I cannot name, I began to implore the Angel to hold off for a few moments, and the world would do penance. But my plea was a mere nothing in the face of the divine anger. Just then I saw the Most Holy Trinity. The greatness of Its majesty pierced me deeply, and I did not dare to repeat my entreaties. At that very moment I felt in my soul the power of Jesus' grace, which dwells in my soul. When I became conscious of this grace, I was instantly snatched up before the Throne of God. Oh, how great is our Lord and God and how incomprehensible His holiness! I will make no attempt to describe this greatness, because before long we shall all see Him as He is. I found myself pleading with God for the world with words heard interiorly.
>
> As I was praying in this manner, I saw the Angel's helplessness: He could not carry out the just punishment which was rightly due for sins. Never before had I prayed with such inner power as I did then (474).

The words that St. Faustina "heard interiorly" were the prayers of the Chaplet of Divine Mercy, which is prayed as follows:

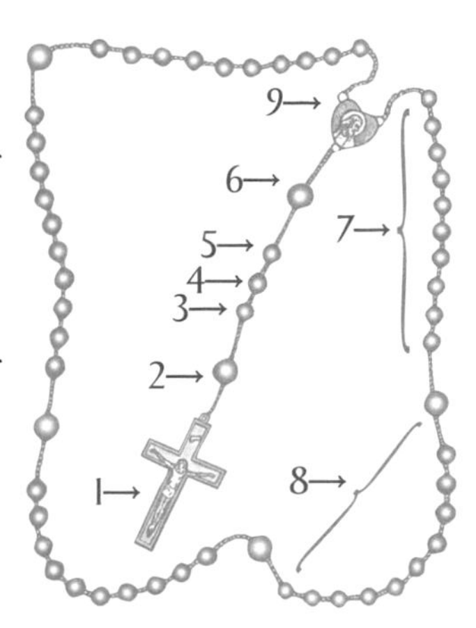

1. Make the Sign of the Cross

2. Optional Opening Prayers
You expired, Jesus, but the source of life gushed forth for souls, and the ocean of mercy opened up for the whole world. O Fount of Life, unfathomable Divine Mercy, envelop the whole world and empty Yourself out upon us. O Blood and Water, which gushed forth from the Heart of Jesus as a fount of Mercy for us, I trust in You.

3. Our Father

4. Hail Mary

5. The Apostle's Creed

6. The Eternal Father
Eternal Father, I offer You the Body and Blood, Soul and Divinity of Your Dearly Beloved Son, Our Lord, Jesus Christ, in atonement for our sins and those of the whole world.

7. On the Ten Small Beads of Each Decade
For the sake of His sorrowful Passion, have mercy on us and on the whole world.

8. Repeat for the remaining four decades
Say the "Eternal Father" (6) on the "Our Father" bead and then 10 "For the sake of His sorrowful Passion" (7) on the following "Hail Mary" beads.

9. Conclude with Holy God
(Repeat three times) Holy God, Holy Mighty One, Holy Immortal One, have mercy on us and on the whole world.

10. Optional Closing Prayer
Eternal God, in whom mercy is endless and the treasury of compassion inexhaustible, look kindly upon us and increase Your mercy in us, that in difficult moments we might not despair nor become despondent, but with great confidence submit ourselves to Your holy will, which is Love and Mercy itself. Amen.

[160] Regarding the power of little souls to save the world, Jesus told St. Faustina: "For your sake I will withhold the hand which punishes; for your sake I bless the earth" (*Diary*, 431). Faustina also shared the following experiences she had in prayer: "I interceded before Him for the whole world. At such moments I have the feeling that the whole world is depending on me" (ibid., 870). And also,

> In one instant the Lord gave me a knowledge of the sins committed throughout the whole world during these days. I fainted from fright, and even though I know the depth of God's mercy, I was surprised that God allows humanity to exist. And the Lord gave me to know who it is that upholds the existence of mankind: it is the chosen souls (ibid., 926).

[161] *Story of a Soul*, p. 214.
[162] Ibid., p. 211.
[163] For a fuller explanation of the dynamic between consolation and desolation and how to remain faith-filled and joyful, see "The Rules for the Discernment of Spirits for Little Souls" in Appendix One of *Consoling the Heart of Jesus: A Do-It-Yourself Retreat Inspired by the Spiritual Exercises of St. Ignatius of Loyola* (Stockbridge: Marian Press, 2010).
[164] See Gaucher, p. 94.
[165] See *Story of a Soul*, p. 270.
[166] Cited in Gaucher, p. 191.
[167] Pope John Paul II, *Theotókos: Woman, Mother, Disciple* (Boston: Pauline Books and Media, 2000), p. 38.
[168] *Catechism*, 399.
[169] *Diary*, 367. Emphasis added.
[170] *Diary*, 86.
[171] Saint John of the Cross, *The Living Flame of Love*, commentary on stanza 1, line 6 (cited in Gaucher, p. 221).
[172] Cited in van Dijk.
[173] *Story of a Soul*, p. 259.
[174] *Letters of St. Thérèse of Lisieux*, vol. 2, p. 999.
[175] The last clause, "and those of the Blessed Mother," is particularly appropriate for those who have consecrated themselves totally to Jesus through Mary. If you have not yet made a Marian consecration, you may still include this clause. However, please consider consecrating yourself to Jesus through Mary soon.
[176] Regarding the clause "through the hands of Mary Immaculate," see previous endnote.
[177] See Ahern, p. 84.
[178] For group recitation, I recommend the Prayer of Consecration to Merciful Love.
[179] *Story of a Soul*, p. 181.
[180] Ibid.
[181] *Story of a Soul*, p. 165.

[182] Again, for group recitation, I recommend the Prayer of Consecration to Merciful Love.
[183] *Story of a Soul*, pp. 276-77.
[184] See, for instance, the Second Vatican Council's Pastoral Constitution on the Church in the Modern World, *Gaudium et Spes* (December 7, 1965) and Declaration on Religious Liberty, *Dignitatis Humanae* (December 7, 1965).
[185] *Story of a Soul*, p. 14.
[186] Ibid.
[187] Cited in *The Power of Confidence*, p. 228.
[188] *Story of a Soul*, p. 180.
[189] In my opinion, the best translation of St. Thérèse's autobiography *Story of a Soul* is by John Clarke, OCD.
[190] See, for example, *Diary*, 611, 651.
[191] Regarding the graces associated with the Image of Divine Mercy, see the following words of Jesus to St. Faustina, recorded in her *Diary*:

> I promise that the soul that will venerate this image will not perish. I also promise victory over [its] enemies already here on earth, especially at the hour of death. I Myself will defend it as My own glory (48).
>
> I am offering people a vessel with which they are to keep coming for graces to the fountain of mercy. That vessel is this image with the signature: "Jesus, I trust in You" (327).
>
> By means of this Image, I shall be granting many graces to souls; so let every soul have access to it (570).
>
> Let the rays of grace enter your soul; they bring with them light, warmth, and life (1486).

[192] Regarding the Image of Divine Mercy, Jesus tells St. Faustina, "Not in the beauty of the color, nor of the brush, lies the greatness of this image, but in My grace" (*Diary*, 313).
[193] See Ahern, p. 84.
[194] While the idea that we can console Jesus the Head of the Mystical Body sometimes causes difficulty for people, the idea that we can console Jesus in the members of his Body is usually *not* a problem. Here's how that is often explained:

> We can console Jesus by giving consolation to the members of his body. In other words, we console Jesus by consoling one another, for we're all members of the Mystical Body of Christ (see 1 Cor 12:12-27). For example, we console Jesus when we alleviate the suffering of the poor, the sick, and the lonely, for they truly are Christ to us. The Lord Jesus himself

> tells us this in Sacred Scripture, "Whatsoever you do to the least of my people, that you do unto me" (Mt 20:25).

[195] See *Consoling the Heart of Jesus*, pp. 46-59.
[196] *Diary*, 244.
[197] Ibid., 1120.
[198] *Catechism*, 467.
[199] See the thorough treatment of the mystery of the heart in Sacred Scripture by Timothy O'Donnell, STD, in *Heart of the Redeemer: An Apologia for the Contemporary and Perennial Value of the Devotion to the Sacred Heart of Jesus* (San Francisco: Ignatius Press, 1989), pp. 23-53.
[200] *Catechism*, 478.
[201] Saint Mother Teresa of Calcutta, whose central desire was to quench the thirst of Jesus and console his Heart, expresses this idea best in her "I thirst" letter, which you can find in *33 Days to Morning Glory*, pp. 70-71. (See also ibid., pp. 81-83 to learn more about how she lived a spirituality of consoling Jesus.)
[202] Pope Pius XI does use the term "console" in his encyclical letter, *Miserentissimus Redemptor*, when he describes how we can make reparation to the Sacred Heart of Jesus:

> Now if, because of our sins also which were as yet in the future, but were *foreseen*, the soul of Christ became sorrowful unto death, it cannot be doubted that then, too, already He derived somewhat of solace from our reparation, which was *likewise foreseen*, when "there appeared to him an angel from heaven" (Lk 22:13), in order that His Heart, oppressed with weariness and anguish, might find consolation. And so even now, in a wondrous yet true manner, *we can and ought to console that Most Sacred Heart which is continually wounded by the sins of thankless men*, since — as we also read in the sacred liturgy — Christ Himself, by the mouth of the Psalmist complains that He is forsaken by His friends: "My Heart hath expected reproach and misery, and I looked for one that would grieve together with me, but there was none: and for one that would comfort me, and I found none" (Ps 68:21) (13, emphasis added).

[203] *Dives in Misericordia*, 7-8.
[204] *Catechism*, 1085. See the full quote, which refers to the Paschal mystery, but has to do with "all that [Christ] did":

> His Paschal mystery is a real event that occurred in our history, but it is unique: all other historical events happened once, and then they pass away, swallowed up in the past. The Paschal mystery of Christ, by contrast, cannot remain only in the past, because by his death he destroyed death, and all that Christ is

> — all that he did and suffered for all men — participates in the divine eternity, and so transcends all times while being made present in them all. The event of the Cross and Resurrection abides and draws everything toward life.

For an in-depth explanation as to how we "get into contact" with these abiding mysteries of Christ's life through faith (which helps explain how we console Jesus when he's "happy in heaven"), see *The One Thing Is Three*, pp. 76-81.

[205] *Catechism*, 478.

[206] Aristotle, *Nicomachean Ethics*, Book VIII, 5, 8.

[207] Karol Wojtyla, cited by George Weigel in *Witness to Hope: The Biography of Pope John Paul II* (New York, NY: HarperCollins Publishers, Inc., 1999), p. 102.

[208] Ibid.

[209] According to Pope John Paul II in his encyclical letter *Dives in Misericordia*, mercy is a "bilateral" reality, a two-way street (14). In other words, it can't be mercy doled out from a high pedestal. Well, amazingly *God allows this principle to apply to his relationship with us in Christ Jesus.* For, again, we have mercy on Jesus by letting him have mercy on us. It's as if Jesus were saying to us, "Would you please have mercy on my Heart by letting me save you, love you, and make you happy?" Here's the full citation from John Paul on mercy as a "bilateral" reality (which, again, applies even to God having mercy on us in Christ):

> We must also continually purify all our actions and all our intentions in which mercy is understood and practiced in a unilateral way, as a good done to others. An act of merciful love is only really such when we are deeply convinced at the moment that we perform it that we are at the same time receiving mercy from the people who are accepting it from us. If this bilateral and reciprocal quality is absent, our actions are not yet true acts of mercy, nor has there yet been fully completed in us that conversion to which Christ has shown us the way by His words and example, even to the Cross, nor are we yet sharing fully in the magnificent source of merciful love that has been revealed to us by Him (14).

[210] *Diary*, 761. Emphasis added. The certainty of victory comes from Jesus' own words, "If only you are willing to fight, know that the victory is always on your side" (ibid., 1560).

[211] See *Summa Theologiae*, III, q. 80, a. 2, s.c. and ad. 3, that is, Part 3 of the *Summa Theologiae*, question 80, article 2, both the main reply and the reply to objection 3:

> *I answer that* ... In another way one may eat Christ spiritually, as He is under the sacramental species, inasmuch as a man

> believes in Christ, while desiring to receive this sacrament; and this is not merely to eat Christ spiritually, but likewise to eat this sacrament; which does not fall to the lot of the angels. And therefore although the angels feed on Christ spiritually, yet it does not belong to them to eat this sacrament spiritually.
>
> *Reply to Obj. 3:* Christ dwells in men through faith ...

[212] See endnote 191.
[213] While I'm using the word "family" here in the traditional sense, other groups of people who live together (without being in the state of sin) could also make this offering. For example, a group of college roommates could make the offering. However, for someone who lives by himself, I would encourage him to make the individual Offering to Merciful Love of St. Thérèse of Lisieux, which this book describes. (Actually, family members can also make that individual 33-day preparation and consecration in conjunction with the Family Offering and Enthronement.) I would also encourage such a person to still do the Divine Mercy Image Enthronement, which I'll explain in the next section.
[214] Sharing God's mercy with others is a key to living the Family Offering to Merciful Love. This highlights the truth that asking for rejected mercy is not a selfish act, and it doesn't take graces away from others. Here's what I mean: If "Family A" rejects the mercy of God and "Family B" receives it and shows mercy to others, then Family B becomes a light to families who have rejected God's mercy, like Family A. In fact, the Merciful Love that comes from Family B to Family A becomes, in a sense, Family A's "second chance" to receive God's mercy. In sum: If Family A rejects God's mercy and Family B receives it, then Family A has a second chance to receive mercy through the mercy that flows through the merciful deeds, words, and prayers of Family B.
[215] *Diary*, 723.
[216] Ibid., 1074.
[217] Ibid., 367.
[218] Ibid., 454.
[219] Ibid., 1017.
[220] Regardless of the day on which this offering is first made, it's a good idea to renew it on Divine Mercy Sunday, which is a day of great grace and the preeminent feast for the devotion to Divine Mercy.
[221] See endnote 191.
[222] *Diary*, 327.
[223] Ibid., 570.
[224] Ibid., 341.

Resource Pages

More from Fr. Gaitley

Y26-CHMB

Consoling the Heart of Mary: Basic Training for Mary's Marines

From the author of *33 Days to Morning Glory* comes a powerful new book that will take you much deeper into living a total consecration to Jesus through Mary. Relying on the rich insights and profound Marian wisdom of St. Maximilian Kolbe, Fr. Gaitley shares how we can all become "Mary's Marines" and help win the world for Christ.

33 Days to Morning Glory*

Begin an extraordinary 33-day journey to Marian consecration with four spiritual giants: Sts. Louis de Montfort, Maximilian Kolbe, Mother Teresa of Calcutta, and John Paul II. (198 pages.)

Y26-33DAY *e*book: **Y26-EB33DAY**

The 'One Thing' Is Three*

Learn the key to the Church's wisdom and the greatest mystery of the Catholic faith: the Most Holy Trinity. (400 pages.) **Y26-ONE** *e*book: **Y26-EBONE**

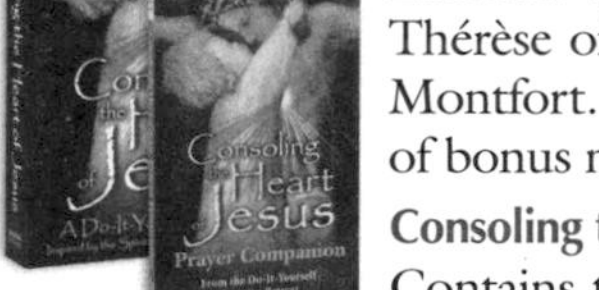

Y26-CHJ *e*book: **Y26-EBCHJ** **Y26-PCCHJ**

Consoling the Heart of Jesus*

This do-it-yourself retreat combines the *Spiritual Exercises of St. Ignatius* with the teachings of Saints Thérèse of Lisieux, Faustina Kowalska, and Louis de Montfort. (428 pages.) Includes more than 200 pages of bonus material.

Consoling the Heart of Jesus Prayer Companion

Contains the essence of Consoling spirituality and all the main prayers from the popular retreat. (126 pages.)

'You Did it to Me': A Practical Guide to Mercy in Action*

"[This book] blew me away. I believe it will become a spiritual classic, right up there with *33 Days to Morning Glory.*"
— David Came, Marian Press

'You Did It to Me:' Putting Mercy into Action

5-part DVD series.
As seen on EWTN.

Y26-2MEDVD

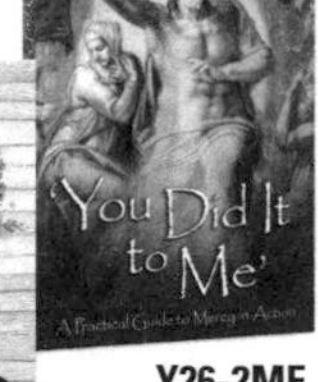

Y26-2ME

*Available as small group programs!

For our complete line of books, prayercards, pamphlets, and more, visit ShopMercy.org or call 1-800-462-7426.

Diary of Saint Maria Faustina Kowalska: Divine Mercy in My Soul

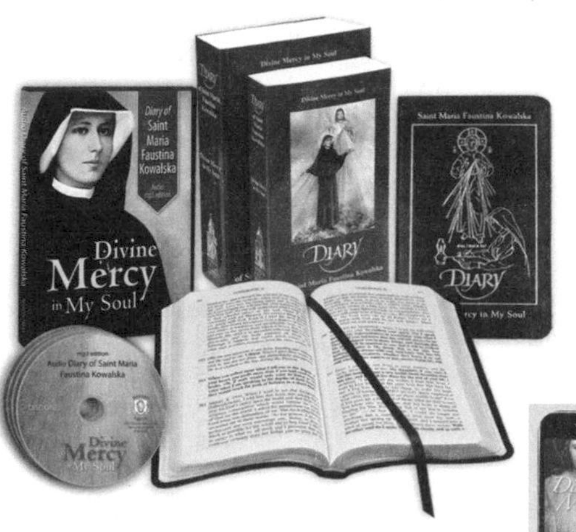

Paperback
Y26-NBFD
Compact Edition
Y26-DNBF
Deluxe Leather-Bound Edition
Y26-DDBURG
Audio Diary Mp3 Edition
Y26-ADMP3
Ebook Diary
Y26-EDIARY

Free Divine Mercy App! Available for Apple and Android mobile devices.

The Second Greatest Story Ever Told*

Father Michael Gaitley, MIC, expounds on the profound connection between Divine Mercy and Marian consecration, culminating in the person of John Paul II. A must-read for all those who desire to bear witness to the mercy of God. **Y26-SGSBK** ebook: **Y26-EBSGSBK**

Divine Mercy in the Second Greatest Story (DVD and Guidebook)

New! Exciting 10-part series with DVD and workbook hosted and written by Fr. Michael Gaitley and based on his bestselling book *The Second Greatest Story Ever Told.*

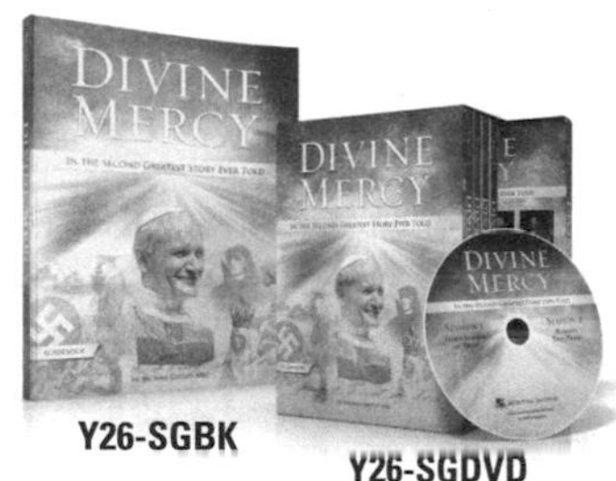

Y26-SGBK **Y26-SGDVD**

DivineMercyArt.com

Top Quality Religious Art … at *Merciful* Prices!

Y26-PIM10GW Y26-PB10GW

Handmade at the National Shrine of The Divine Mercy with top-quality wood, canvas, and inks.

- Lowest prices
- Gallery wrap
- Framing options

DivineMercyArt.com or call 1-800-462-7426

Prices subject to change.

Hearts Afire: Parish-based Programs (HAPP®)

from the Marian Fathers of the Immaculate Conception

STAGE ONE: The Two Hearts

PART 1: The Immaculate Heart

We begin our journey to the Immaculate Heart with the book *33 Days to Morning Glory* and its accompanying group-retreat program.

PART 2: The Sacred Heart

Mary then leads us to the Sacred Heart, which begins the second part of Stage One with the book *Consoling the Heart of Jesus* and its accompanying group-retreat program.

STAGE TWO: Wisdom & Works of Mercy

We begin Stage Two with *The 'One Thing' Is Three* and its accompanying group-study program, which gives group members a kind of crash course in Catholic theology. Stage Two concludes with a program for group works of mercy based on *'You Did It to Me.'*

STAGE THREE: Keeping the Hearts Afire

The heart of Stage Three is the **Marian Missionaries of Divine Mercy**, which invites participants to concretely live everything they've learned in the Hearts Afire program and continue their formation with additional group programs such as the 33 Days to Merciful Love Group Retreat and the *Divine Mercy in the Second Greatest Story Ever Told* series. Become a Marian Missionary: MarianMissionaries.org, 413-944-8500.

HAPP: 1-844-551-3755
Orders: 1-800-462-7426
AllHeartsAfire.org
HAPP@marian.org

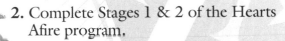